Other books by Pam Johnson-Bennett

Think Like a Cat

Psycho Kitty

Starting from Scratch

Cat vs. Cat

Hiss and Tell

Twisted Whiskers

Read Pam and Kae's blog at
www.twoloonsandabook.com

Cookies for Dinner

Cookies for Dinner

The tales of two moms in their quest to survive motherhood

Pam Johnson-Bennett and Kae Allen

White River Press
Amherst, Massachusetts

First published 2011

White River Press, PO Box 3561, Amherst, MA 01004

www.whiteriverpress.com

ISBN: 978-1-935052-51-7 paperback
ISBN: 978-1-935052-52-4 eBook

Author photo: Christi Allen

Cover design: Dave Aldrich, aldrichdesgin.com

Illustration: Susan Carter

Library of Congress Cataloging-in-Publication Data

Johnson-Bennett, Pam, 1954-
Cookies for dinner : the tales of two moms in their quest to survive motherhood / Pam Johnson-Bennett and Kae Allen.
    p. cm.
ISBN 978-1-935052-51-7 (pbk. : alk. paper) — ISBN 978-1-935052-52-4 (ebook)
1. Johnson-Bennett, Pam, 1954- 2. Allen, Kae, 1963- 3. Motherhood. 4. Parenting. 5. Mothers—United States. I. Allen, Kae, 1963- II. Title.
HQ759.J675 2011
306.874'3—dc22
                        2011015917

Dedicated to Scott, Gracie, and Jack with all my love.

Dedicated to David, Matt, Christi and Jess,
you are my heart and soul.

Phone Conversation

Pam: Whew! We finally finished this book. I've learned a lot about you that I didn't know.

Kae: Yeah, me too. In fact, I think you're a lunatic.

Pam: *Me?* I don't think so. You're the lunatic.

Kae: I have never had to duct-tape my child's diaper closed.

Pam: You put your husband in time-out.

Kae: You vacuumed during a tornado.

Pam: Do I need to bring up your little sausage and egg biscuit secret?

Kae: You got locked out of your house in your swimsuit.

Pam: You hosed your son down in his car seat on the front lawn.

Kae: That was an emergency. You're still a lunatic.

Pam: You're a lunatic.

Kae: You want to have lunch today?

Pam: Sounds great. I'll meet you in an hour.

Contents

Cookies for Dinner

Introduction

Meet Pam

I'm Pam. Let me start off by saying that I'm a cat expert. Yes, a cat expert. I'm a certified cat behavior consultant and I know a lot about why cats do the things they do. I've written seven books on the subject. Cats don't confuse me. Kids? They're mind-boggling. I'm a mother, but just when I think I'm beginning to understand my children, I quickly realize that I'm not even close to figuring them out. I am in no way an expert on children. In fact, I often feel I'm in over my head when it comes to what's going on in those little minds.

So why would I want to co-write a book about children and motherhood? Because nothing else in my life gives me as much joy, love, frustration, laughter, and amazement, as my two kids. They have a way of making me feel like the most loved person on the planet one minute, and then can turn around and put life into perspective by telling me that my butt wiggles too much when I walk. They run into my arms to hug and kiss me and it melts away all my tension in a heartbeat. Moments later they are standing with their fingers wagging at me, declaring that they're old enough to decide that sandals are appropriate footwear in the snow. What else in life provides such a roller-coaster ride?

According to my kids, I'm the most beautiful woman in the world with big feet. It doesn't get any better than that. According to my daughter, I'm the smartest mommy in the world until I let it slip that I didn't remember her *new* favorite color is purple. Luckily, she's young enough that I can win back her favor with a couple of cookies. I'm not above bribery. Oh, I'm sure child experts have exhausted that subject, and it's probably very well known among the *good* parents that you shouldn't bribe your children to be good. In my opinion, though, I'm in the trenches and it's every mom for herself. If a cookie gets me out of the mommy doghouse, I'm going for it. I'm not proud. In fact, these days I'm not well-groomed, well-rested, well-dressed, or well-read. I am, however, well-stocked. Need a cookie? I'm your girl.

Even though I often feel way over my head when it comes to being a parent, I'm fortunate to have a very good friend, Kae Allen, who has already made it through the motherhood jungle and come out the other side with nothing but a few bug bites. The paths we took to motherhood were very different, as you'll read in this book, but we learned that no matter how we got on the ride, at some point we all end up standing in the checkout line at Walmart, exchanging potty training horror stories with total strangers.

My journey into motherhood came rather late in my life. I was 47 years old. My journey into motherhood also came by way of adoption. Although adoption grants a more mature woman the opportunity to experience being the mother of an infant, I have to admit that I wasn't completely prepared for the one teeny weeny little bug in my well-thought-out dream—*menopause*. I never realized how much heat a baby can generate until I rocked my daughter to sleep in my arms while having a hot flash. It was also quite an experience to try to get to know a completely unfamiliar human being while your own body is acting like a stranger. Ahh, yes, hormones. You fix your hair perfectly and apply makeup and moments later the hormones from hell turn up the heat. You are transformed into a frizzy-haired, makeup-smeared mad woman who wildly runs around opening windows or sticking your head in the refrigerator.

In my early 20s I was informed by several doctors that I was unable to ever give birth. The realization that I would never be a mother was devastating. I endured countless visits to fertility experts and numerous unflattering procedures where total strangers got views of me even I've never seen. It all failed anyway, and my ovaries were declared dead as a doornail. At the time, I was not in the healthiest of marriages, so after allowing myself to grieve, I tried to view this news as a way of finding a path out of the marriage. I cried, I mourned, and then I got divorced.

I turned my attention toward my career and was careful to keep my heartbreak buried deep inside. Whenever I felt myself mourning the lost dream of motherhood, I would push it out of my head. To banish the desire for children, I would look around me at all the inconveniences of motherhood. I'd drive around in my cute little Mustang while watching mothers lug their kids in and out of boxy station wagons and minivans. I'd sit in an airplane seat while a child behind me performed the ritualistic kicking of my seatback (there must be a child manual somewhere that adults aren't allowed to read that states seat kicking is a rite of passage). I'd turn around in my seat and look at the frustrated face of the seat-kicker's mother, so grateful that I was not the one who had to endure that child 24/7.

If seat kicking didn't manage to reconfirm my joy of being childless, I'd go to restaurants, where I could enjoy my meal without interruption. I didn't have to cut anyone's meat, take anyone to the potty eight times in 20 minutes, nor did I have to warn my pint-sized dining companions not to shove peas up their noses or throw food.

Yet, despite all the fun I was having as a woman unencumbered by children, those motherhood pangs continued to resurface. Even though I ditched the husband and had found my career calling, I still painfully yearned for a little seat-kicking, food-throwing, pea-shover of my very own. But with no husband, and nearing the end of my 30s, it didn't look as if I'd ever have a reason to buy a minivan or tell my dining companions not to throw food. (Well, actually, that's not exactly accurate; some of my dates did have terrible table manners—but that's another book.)

Fate has such a sense of humor, though. I entered my 40s, my career became solid, and I happily resigned myself to the path I was on. *That's* when everything turned upside down and I met a wonderful man, fell deeply in love, and got married. Even though I viewed myself as damaged goods, my new husband, Scott, helped me find my heart again. I have to say that opposites must truly attract. I have OCD and have been on a mission to clean the world since I was a teenager. Scott, on the other hand, has a live-and-let-live attitude when it comes to dirt, disarray, and unwashed dishes. Other couples might have found these differences to be a deal-breaker but for some twisted, inexplicable reason, we are a perfect match.

Five years into the marriage, those seat-kicking, pea-shoving, food-throwing thoughts crept back into my head, and this time there was no pushing them away. Hormones and dried-up ovaries be damned, I was going to be a mother...somehow. So we began the adoption process. By the way, if you ever feel as if your life is too private and you long for complete strangers to know every aspect of your existence, from how much you weigh to how much you make, what's in your closet, what kind of pajamas you sleep in (or whether you sleep in pajamas at all), and what your friends *really* think of you, go through the adoption process.

Adoption takes you to places in your own little town where you never thought you'd be. It was quite an eye-opener for me to be standing in line at our county jail to be fingerprinted, while prisoners waved to me from their cells. This fun little experience is part of the criminal background check required for prospective adoptive parents. I'm certainly glad that prospective parents are thoroughly checked out, but being at the fingerprint station of my county jail did not figure into my little romantic dream of how to become a mother. In fact, while we're being honest here, I plan on using this experience with my children, if needed. Since I can't use the guilt of how many hours of labor I endured, I admit I won't be above reminding them that I stood on line with scary-looking inmates while waiting to be fingerprinted in jail...*twice.* (I have two kids.)

Nine months after starting the adoption process, we received word from our adoption agency that our little daughter was born in Guatemala. I have to admit that after the unbelievably draining process of being approved for an adoption, I was more than ready to get on that plane, fly to Guatemala, and begin being a mother. After all, I had postponed this long enough. I was now Gracie's mother. I had a daughter. I was about to live my dream.

Okay, now remember when I said I wanted to experience being the mother of a seat-kicking, pea-shoving, food thrower? Well, nowhere did I mention that I was prepared for a crying...no, let me rephrase that...*screaming* infant who hated the very sight of me. From the moment Gracie was placed in my arms, she screamed. This wasn't the way it was supposed to be! She was supposed to look up at me, fall instantly in love, and we were to start our wonderful life together as mother and daughter. Intellectually, I knew it would take time for Gracie to bond with me and it was normal for her to be stressed. Emotionally though, I wanted Madonna and child. At the very least, I wanted her to not view me as the devil. There I was, in a hotel room in Guatemala at two in the morning, with an infant in my arms who looked at me with total panic. What had I done?

In writing this book and reflecting back on that time, I realize that no matter what all the childcare experts say, when it comes right down to it, you go on love, instinct, and fear. You make it up as you go along, hoping your kids won't end up on a therapist's couch spilling the beans about having a lunatic for a mother. Kae's kids have all turned out great, and so far she hasn't confessed to me about any huge therapist bills. As for my kids, they'll still young, so there are plenty of opportunities for me to create memories that will help some future therapist make his Mercedes payments.

This book is by no means a guide to proper motherhood. If that's what you're looking for, put this book back on the shelf and step away quickly. However, if you're looking for reassurance that there are other mothers out there who feel just as crazy and over-whelmed as you, then we're your girls and this is the book for you!

Meet Kae

My name is Kae. I am a middle-aged accountant who likes to bowl. I have raised three wonderful, well-adjusted children who have been gracious enough to allow me to write stories about their lives. With regard to children, I am currently in the limbo land between raised children and grandchildren. After 27 years of raising children, I am basking in the glow of empty nest syndrome. My husband, David, and I enjoy playing golf, traveling, and spoiling our female Goldendoodle dog, Fred.

The reason I am writing this book goes back 15 years ago when Scott, "our worker man" (as proclaimed by our youngest child, Jessica), became a fixture in our house for several months. Scott was the head carpenter on a large remodeling job and became one of our friends. Scott was single at the time and spent evenings with us eating dinner and debating politics with my husband. After the remodeling job was finished, Scott hired me to be his accountant and put the tattered pieces of his financial world in order. Several years later, Scott met Pam and the budding romance became a marriage. We were thrilled for Scott. He is a wonderful person who deserves to have a wonderful wife. Pam is smart and pretty and, most of all, made Scott's eyes light up.

A few years later, we were filling out paperwork to help Scott and Pam adopt their first child. It was a pensive and exciting time for them both. Once Gracie was on the scene, Pam would tell me about the latest goings on with her baby daughter. Sometimes it was the difficulty of getting her to sleep all night, sometimes how to keep her in her clothes, sometimes how she was throwing temper tantrums like it was her job. The common theme was that motherhood was leaving Pam feeling exhausted and insecure about her abilities. I would usually regale her with one of my stories of how you don't have to be perfect to be a mother, and she would feel much better.

One tax season, sitting over their federal 1040 form, Scott brought up the idea of Pam and me writing a book together. Pam is a published author. I am an accountant. This didn't really sound like a good idea. So I declined.

One year later, once again sitting over the federal 1040 form, after giving them the annual update on the Allen children, the subject of a book was brought up again. Not by me. Once again, it didn't seem like a good idea, so I declined. I am a bean counter by trade. I can tell my stories about the children to my clients because they are a captive audience until I tell them how much the damage is and where to sign. You, dear reader, have to actually plunk down some of your hard-earned cash to hear one of my "kids are a snick" stories.

One more year went by and, once again sitting over the federal 1040 form, the subject was brought up. This time I said I would think about it. In the next two months I had three people tell me that I should write a book. No sledgehammer needed. I called Pam and said I was in. And that is how this whole thing got started.

My journey into adulthood/motherhood was a bit on the rough side. I was married at the age of 19 and wanted nothing more than to settle down and raise a family in the proverbial house with the white picket fence. Things went along as planned. I got married, bought a nice house, and started working on having a family. The concept of getting pregnant seems pretty straightforward, but we somehow kept missing the mark. Eventually, after several months of trying, we succeeded. The baby was on the way and life was perfect. Morning sickness was something I read about but never had. My pregnancy was progressing perfectly and there was nothing but bluebirds and rainbows in the land of Kae. That is, until I got a phone call in the middle of the night from someone's irate boyfriend. This is when I found out that "fishing with the guys" was really code for "spending the night with my girlfriend." I came to find out my husband had been leaving love notes on the back of his business card on the windshield of his girlfriend's car. We all do some stupid things in life, but let me give a word of advice to all the adulterers out there: If you don't want to get caught, don't write love notes on the back of your business card! And for all the adulterers' love interests: Don't leave the business cards where your boyfriend can find them!

In the wee hours of a Saturday morning, my land of happy ever after in the house with the white picket fence evaporated. My husband and I talked about working things out, but it was hard when he was still seeing the girlfriend. But honestly, that is not what ended the marriage. It was one simple question I asked him: "Where do you want to be when you are 40 years old?" I won't bore you with his answer, but suffice it to say he loaded up his truck and moved in with his girlfriend that day. Better her than me to end up where he wanted to be.

Going through a pregnancy and a divorce at the same time was emotionally difficult, but I was lucky to have good friends who pushed and prodded me through the tough times. One of my core beliefs is that everything happens for a reason and you will see the reason if you just wait for it. It was during this time in my life that this philosophy was born. The next year and a half was a downward spiral that I don't care to recount in any great detail. Suffice it to say that when bad decisions are made, bad events are sure to follow.

Fortunately for me, during this time I met a wonderful man. We would go to dinner and talk for hours and hours and hours. It always seemed when I was down and feeling sorry for myself I would open the mailbox and find a letter from David. When he was in law school he would write me long letters while sitting in the penguin house at the Lincoln Park Zoo in Chicago. When Matthew was born, David was in town but I hadn't been able to see him because he had a cold. He drove all the way to the hospital just to look through the glass and see my son. He then flew back to Chicago, jumped in his car, and sped all the way to South Bend, Indiana, before the bookstore at Notre Dame University closed for the day. (There must be some mind-altering experience that happens when you attend Notre Dame. The alumni are zealots, and David is no different.) The next day, when I was overwhelmed with being alone with Matthew for the first time, the doorbell rang. It was the FedEx delivery man with a box for me. Inside was everything Notre Dame sold for a baby. There were booties, bibs, a little blue jacket with "Fighting Irish" on it and a matching set of shorts and pants, a little stocking cap, and too many other things to remember.

Nine months after Matthew was born, my life hit rock bottom. The world I was living in was crazy and abusive. Finally I woke up and realized that I might not be worth much, but Matthew sure as poop deserved a lot better than to be raised in this chaotic mess I was calling my life. Once again, fate placed David at my doorstep the day I was deciding whether to move to Tennessee to be closer to my dad or to California to be closer to my brother. David asked me to move to Chicago with him. Just as friends, you understand. We could get an apartment together (perfectly platonic), and he would help me with the bills and Matthew. I figured that if I was going to jump off a cliff, I might as well get a running start. So I packed up all my worldly possessions and moved to a western suburb of Chicago called Western Springs. It was in the embrace of David's family that I finally learned what happiness is. Happiness is calm, quiet, and amazingly sane.

A year later, I was standing at the end of the aisle in the Presbyterian Church of Western Springs. Considering what had become of my earlier attempt at marriage made me somewhat nervous. What if I made a mistake? I turned the corner into the church and standing at the end of the aisle was David, so handsome in his tuxedo, holding Matthew in his arms, wearing the exact same tuxedo, slurping juice out of his favorite blue bottle. That was the exact moment I knew we were back in the land of bluebirds and rainbows for Kae.

The summer after Jessica was born, we moved to Murfreesboro, Tennessee. David established his own law practice and I attended Middle Tennessee State University to finish the last three classes I needed to complete my accounting degree.

I have been married to David for more than two decades. We live in an antebellum house with a little white picket fence. David is my husband, my best friend, and my soul mate. Without him, I would be only a portion of the person I have become. Together, and sometimes in spite of each other, we have raised three happy, healthy, and emotionally stable children.

In writing this down and thinking about what each child needed in the first five years of their lives, there was no one easy child and no one hard child. Matthew put me through my parental paces in his own way, but he was also a wonderfully easy child to raise. Christina, who would be up for the easiest child to raise award, still put me through the wringer as a parent—just on a different front. Jessica was enormously easy to handle as far as discipline was concerned, until she learned to talk. But she required constant parental attention because she was hell bent on running before she learned to walk.

Raising the children was the most important thing I will ever do. It was exasperating, exhilarating, and sometimes messy and gross. But it was also great fun.

I hope these stories about my journey into motherhood give you encouragement and solace. And just for the record, as of this writing, I have yet to spend any of my retirement funds on therapy bills for the children.

Chapter 1

The Journey Begins

Pam's Flight to Motherhood

By Pam

I first met my daughter in 2002 in an old hotel in Guatemala. My four-month-old baby girl was placed in my arms by her foster mother. Also present were my husband, our Guatemalan lawyer, and a translator.

Gracie was dressed in a beautiful little dress and had a bow in her hair. Her gorgeous little face, however, was puffy, distorted, and red from nonstop screaming. She had been with the foster mother since her birth and was not thrilled at being handed over to me. In fact, I hadn't ever recalled hearing a baby wail as horribly as this little child. The translator assured me this was normal and that Gracie would warm up to me in an hour or so. That, however, would not be the case.

My first night with Gracie consisted of me sitting on the edge of the bed, gently rocking her in the rickety old cradle provided by the hotel. Her screams would come and go, but when they came, boy, I sure felt sorry for the other guests. Luckily, this was a hotel where many other adoptive parents were also in similar situations, though I would learn later that most of them were silently saying prayers of thanks that the screaming banshee in Room Six didn't belong to them.

1

Minutes turned into hours. I gently stroked my new daughter's hair when she was in one of the non-screaming phases. Scott slept soundly on the bed. How he did that, I still don't know. I'm wondering whether someone from the hotel staff secretly supplied new fathers with ear plugs. Apparently, the wee hours of the morning were strictly for mommies.

I looked at my precious daughter as she finally gave in to her exhaustion and I whispered, "I love you." I wasn't in a clean hospital, giving birth, surrounded by family—I was in a run-down, hot, stuffy Guatemalan hotel, sitting on the edge of a bed that should've been thrown out years ago, watching my daughter sleep while a line of ants walked up and over my toes. It was the happiest moment of my life.

I leaned over the cradle and ever so gently kissed Gracie. The feeling of love that swept over me exceeded anything I thought a human was capable of. I said goodnight to the Guatemalan ants and went to bed. *I was a mother.*

The next morning we began the journey home to the United States. I took the time to do my hair nicely, apply makeup, and put on the special outfit I had packed for this once-in-a-lifetime event. I dressed Gracie in her own special little outfit that said "Daddy's Girl" on it. I wanted to make sure our pictures from this day would look spectacular.

Our taxi driver arrived earlier than expected and insisted that we leave for the airport right away because traffic was bad. I tossed the camera in my purse without getting any pictures of us all dressed up, but I wasn't worried because we'd have plenty of time at the airport.

Outside in the hotel parking lot, I looked at the cab in which I was to place my precious new family. The best description I can offer is duct tape. It seemed to be holding every part of the car together. There was duct tape around the headlights, tail lights, door handles, and rear bumper. The interior must've had leather or vinyl at some point, but it was now just layer upon layer of duct tape. There I stood with my newly adopted four-month-old daughter in my arms. Oh, did I mention that there are no infant car seats in Guatemala and there's no need for them, since most cars don't have seat belts? So as my husband helped the taxi driver load all our luggage into the duct-tape-lined trunk, I positioned myself on the duct tape in the back seat with my precious daughter clutched in my arms. I then instructed my husband to wedge himself next to me to limit the amount of bouncing and tossing that I might do during transit. He was also instructed to keep his arms tightly around me, since my arms would be wrapped around Gracie.

I used to complain about traffic. I used to complain about being stuck in my car on the interstate behind a sea of red tail lights. Then I went to Guatemala and experienced the freestyle driving of many of that country's citizens. See that Stop sign there? That doesn't mean you actually have to stop. See that pedestrian there? Don't worry, he'll get out of the way. Looking for your seat belt? Don't bother, there aren't any!

This was all relatively fine with me on the way from the Guatemala airport to my hotel (I was once a teenage driver, so some of those maneuvers brought back memories). But the return trip to the airport was very different. The stakes were much higher; *I was a mother.*

I was determined that no matter how fast this driver took the curves and turns, my daughter and I weren't going to budge. What I neglected to take into account, though, was a little something else that *would* budge...the contents of my daughter's stomach. She had every right to heave her breakfast as we rounded turns at tire-squealing speed, but somehow I thought she would've inherited the Guatemalan driving-tolerant digestive system from her biological parents.

Without warning, Gracie's stomach contents made a hasty exit from her system. The word "projectile" took on new meaning for me at that moment. My face, hair, shirt, and bra became victims of the launch, as did Gracie's brand-new outfit. The embroidered "Daddy's Girl" was totally obliterated.

As I look back on things, I know I wasn't adequately prepared for travel because I thought a mere burp cloth neatly slung over my shoulder would protect me from any little spits and burps my perfect little child would release. I still don't understand how a tiny baby can spew forth more than her body weight in vomit. Lesson learned: No matter how much of a rush you're in, *always* take pictures before you leave the building. Second lesson learned: Don't wear dark clothes when your baby is still on formula. Oh yeah, one other lesson: Don't waste money on those cute little burp cloths. Cover yourself from neck to waist in industrial-strength material. Don't shop in the baby department—shop at Home Depot.

Carefully sliding Gracie into my husband's arms, I rummaged through the diaper bag for the remaining few teeny-weeny burp cloths. I gently cleaned my daughter off, then wiped her down with baby wipes. Due to safety concerns, she would have to stay in her vomit-soaked clothes until we could come to a full stop. That happened soon enough as we hit the much-anticipated traffic. I changed Gracie out of her beautiful outfit and into one of the extra one-piece outfits I'd thrown in my bag. Then I turned my attention to my own vomit-enhanced self. All of my carefully applied makeup was wiped off onto a cloth—vomit is a very speedy makeup remover. I finished off by using the aloe vera–enriched baby wipes on my hair. Baby wipes are so versatile, but the one thing they don't do well is leave your hairstyle intact. My hair was now coated, limp, and greasy looking. Yeah, I sure wish I had gotten those pictures before. Much to the taxi driver's rearview mirror entertainment, I reached inside my shirt and tried to remove some vomit from between my breasts.

After the clean-up, we sat in traffic. We sat...and we sat...and we sat. It was hot, and if you're sitting in a duct-taped car with no seat belts you can pretty much be assured that there's no air-conditioning as well. Vomit and heat are not good companions.

My husband, who managed to hold my daughter during the clean-up without getting so much as one droplet on him, turned to me and said, "You really stink."

"I'm well aware of that!" I answered in a tone that caused the taxi driver to momentarily stop looking at my breasts in the mirror.

Arrival at the airport didn't come a moment too soon. Bathroom, where's the bathroom? I wanted to get to a sink as quickly as possible.

"There's no time," my husband told me while pointing to the long line ahead of us. It looked as if *everyone* was leaving the country at the same time. There were forms to fill out, luggage to be opened and inspected, tickets to check, identification to be verified, other lines to stand in, other forms to fill out, and not a lot of room to do it in. *Okay,* I thought, *I'll just wait until we get to our gate. I'm a mother; I can handle this.*

To this day, I still don't understand how this next event could logically take place, but even though Gracie had vomited up everything in her stomach, she still had more surprises up her sleeve... or rather, down south in her diaper. I thought we had a deal: From the moment I first changed her diaper in the hotel room, she was politely presenting me with normal mustard-like baby-appropriate poop. Not fun to change, but definitely well within the spectrum of what I expected. After all, I had read the books, been around friends with babies, and as an adult, I was no stranger to poop. I knew the incoming food had to have an outgoing option. But since she was only on formula, her poop was relatively manageable. For a new mother, this is very much appreciated. In the airport, as we were rushing to our gate, Gracie decided to change the conditions of our deal. Gracie had diarrhea. Gracie had lots of diarrhea. As we were walking, my new mommy nose hairs started twitching and I knew something was brewing in her nether region, but before I could even open my mouth to alert Scott that a bathroom detour was crucial, I felt the telltale leakage coming from around the elastic of Gracie's diaper.

Finally we found a bathroom with too long of a line and too many mothers waiting with screaming babies. They weren't going to be sympathetic to my plight. It was every mother for herself here. *Okay Pam, look around, use your new mommy survival skills.* I spotted an empty table near security.

"Follow me, Scott," I said to my husband and raced over to claim the empty spot. With newly acquired mommy-lightning speed, I grabbed the changing pad, placed Gracie on it, and started stripping her soiled clothes off.

"Here?" asked Scott, as he looked around at the hundreds of people walking by.

"Here!" I stated. "Now get me a clean diaper and open the container of wipes." Oooh, being a mommy was making me feel powerful. Or maybe it was just that the smell of dried formula vomit was affecting my brain. Either way, I was not going to wear any more remnants of bodily functions than I had to. I knew I was going to look rotten in our "welcome home" pictures, but I sure wasn't going to smell rotten as well.

With the crisis averted, I changed Gracie into the final extra outfit from her diaper bag and said a little prayer that the remainder of the trip would be uneventful. I had lots of extra clothes for her but they were all in the checked luggage, so we were on borrowed time from this moment on. If things got any worse, Gracie would be meeting her new grandparents in Nashville wearing only a diaper.

Once onboard the plane, I had to wait until it was safe to leave my seat before I could go into the lavatory to assess my own condition. Gracie was very accommodating and fell asleep in Scott's arms. I kept my fingers crossed that she would remain sleeping, or at least quiet, for the entire flight. I headed to the lavatory. I have never been the type of woman who carries makeup in my purse. One half-melted lipstick is all you'll usually find hidden in there for emergencies. I had the pathetic pink tube with me, but when I looked in the lavatory mirror, I realized that a pink lipsticked mouth would only add to the disaster. It would be best not to try to draw attention to myself, so I rinsed a few strands of my hair in the miniscule sink, washed my face and chest, and emerged from the lavatory with the confidence that one should have when wearing the intriguing scents of vomit, aloe vera, and antibacterial soap.

I was exhausted and looking forward to closing my eyes while Gracie was quiet. I slid down in my seat and leaned my head back. Ahhh, in a few hours I'd be home in Nashville with my new daughter. I was a mommy.

"What's that smell? Is that? Oh, no, not again," I said as the very familiar odor wafted up from my pretty little baby's hind end. "Quick, give her to me," I instructed Scott with the authority of a quarterback calling for the football with time running out. I stood up in the aisle. There were people walking up and down. Why were there so many people in my way? Didn't they realize the pilot had said that unless they had to get up they should stay in their seats? Don't these people listen? Some were reaching up into the overhead bins. Others were milling around talking to people in rows ahead of them. I didn't care if families couldn't sit together. They can talk *after* the plane lands. Right now they stood between me and the bathroom. I had a baby in my arms who was about to let the poop fly and I had no extra clothes. I was going to get to the lavatory and that was that. Time to score a touchdown.

I'm normally a very polite person, but impending poop changes everything. I realize I may have stepped on a few toes or pushed past people with less than the best manners, but I was a mommy on a mission. They were all in dry, nice-smelling clothes (most of them, anyway) and I was fighting for apparel survival here.

"Excuse me, pooping baby coming through," I said to everyone as I passed by. I didn't speak Spanish but was hoping that "poop" was one of those universal words everyone understands.

Airplane lavatory changing stations are very amusing. You're supposed to put the baby on the fold-down shelf over the toilet while you're also wrangling the wipes and other paraphernalia needed to clean up the mess down south. While you're attempting this, keep in mind that the plane is in motion and, if you're extra lucky like me, you'll hit turbulence the whole time. Gracie slid from one end of the changing table to the other and hit her head on the wall. She wasn't hurt, but of course it terrified me because I thought she was going to fall into the toilet. I also noticed her take in one of those frighteningly long and silent deep breaths that indicate a *huge* scream is about to occur. You know those breaths. The baby sucks in as much air as possible in order to let out the loudest and longest scream in history. Couple that with the environment of a tiny airplane lavatory and you have a panicky new mommy with a big earache.

I managed to change Gracie without causing further damage, and nothing unintentional went down the toilet. I was, however, nervous about opening the lavatory door and inflicting the ear-shattering noise on my fellow passengers. I was a brand new mommy... what's the mommy protocol? Act apologetic? Act casual? Run? Stay in the lavatory for the remainder of the flight? Think, Pam, think. Are you going to let a little fact like having the baby slide on the changing table in a moving airplane and almost landing in the toilet make you afraid to face the world? Not this new mommy. So I stood up straight, looked in the mirror, arranged my greasy, dirty hair into a makeshift style with my one free hand, and then dug in my pocket for the half-melted tube of pink lipstick. I figured everything would look brighter with pink lips. Gracie and I emerged from the lavatory and I confidently strode back to my seat. I was beginning to get the hang of this motherhood thing. Bring on the camera—I was ready for pictures!

Kae's Journey to Motherhood

By Kae

The journey to motherhood began for me with the closing of a door.

I went into labor with my first child on October 25, 1983, four months after my soon-to-be-ex-husband moved out to live with his girlfriend, six months after my 20th birthday and precisely the morning that I was having my house tented for ticks. Yes, ticks.

There was a retirement center being developed on the land directly behind my house. When the forest was bulldozed, the ticks that lived on the woodland animals came into my yard to feed on my German Shepherd. Ticks are unbelievably invasive. One day I found two ticks on my dog. I called the mobile groomer and set up an appointment for the next week. By the time the groomer came, the ticks were literally eating the poor dog alive. She never came back into the house that day. I called the veterinarian and had her boarded until all the ticks were off her and the infection in her blood was cured. Then she went to stay with some friends. The veterinarian informed me that as long as she was there as a food source the ticks would stay. We were in a tick war zone and I didn't want my dog to become a casualty. The problem was, once the outside food source was gone the ticks invaded my house.

One morning I was sitting on my screened porch drinking coffee and looked up into the corner of the porch where the wall meets the ceiling. Spiders had built a dense web that stretched about nine inches or so to each side. I made a note to knock it down that afternoon and left for work. When I came home from work there were two dense webs, the original one in the corner and a smaller one out along the wall. The telephone rang or something and I became distracted and forgot all about knocking the webs down. Several days later I noticed that the dense webbing now extended from corner to corner on the far end of the porch.

I went around the house and got the garden house. If the spiders had set up camp in my screened porch then it was probably time for a good scrub. Just for the record, one indicator of an upcoming labor event is the insatiable desire to scrub everything in sight. This last week of my pregnancy you could lick any surface in my house to your little heart's content. It was in this hormone-induced nesting aggression that I attacked the porch. I took all the patio furniture out into the yard and hosed it down, then pulled the barbeque grill out into the yard and washed it down with soapy water. I actually shined the cover with car wax because I thought it looked dull. Now for the spider webs. I put the spray nozzle on full blast and sent a laser sharp bead of water directly into the crack where ceiling meets wall, obliterating the webbing, and watched it fall rather heavily to the ground. The sound of the saturated webbing hitting the ground was like a soaked bath towel dropped from the ceiling onto a concrete floor.

Now, I am not a student of arachnological studies, nor do I know the nesting habits of your average garden variety spider. What I do know is that no spider web I had ever seen would make that kind of plopping noise. The water dripping off the ceiling made the mass appear to be moving. Armed with garden hose on full-blast stream mode, ready to defend my bare, swollen feet, I approached the saturated clump of debris. Upon closer inspection I saw that this was no spider web or colony of garden variety spiders. This was a living, moving clump of light brown, round, bloated insects that were now spreading out across my porch in all directions. These were *ticks*!

I waddled into the house as fast as a nine-months-pregnant woman on wet patio pebbles can waddle and grabbed two cans of Raid from under my kitchen sink. Returning to the porch with a can of Raid in each hand, I did my best gun slinger imitation, blasting streams of insecticide at everything that moved. Then I called the exterminator and convinced him to be at my house at eight the very next morning.

I wasn't due for six days, so I thought I had plenty of time to resolve the tick issue before the baby came. Wrong! I met the exterminator at the door with my overnight hospital bag in my hand, praying my water wouldn't break during the negotiations. This was not working out well.

I remember thinking in the last few weeks before my child was born that I couldn't wait for this pregnancy to be over so things would get back to normal—"normal" for me being a soon-to-be-divorced woman with a newborn and a house full of ticks. I wasn't actually asking for much. I wanted to be able to get out of the car without holding onto the top of the window and hoisting myself up. I wanted to go to a movie and not have to go to the bathroom half a dozen times. I wanted to pick a chair to sit in because it was comfortable, not because I knew I would be able to get out of it unattended. I wanted to be able to sneeze with the confidence that I would not wet myself or break my water. I wanted to stop crying at Hallmark commercials on TV. I wanted to see my feet. I wanted to wear pants that did not have an elastic panel in the front and leg holes the size of my waist. I wanted to sleep the entire night without being kicked in the bladder, creating the instant need to go to the bathroom. I wanted my belly button to go back to the "innie" it was before my seventh month, instead of the "outie" it had become. I wanted things to get back to *normal*.

When I was in the hospital for two days, I kept thinking, *I can't wait to get home so things will get back to normal.* Lesson quickly learned: Once you have a child, *nothing* is ever normal again.

The day I brought my first child home from the hospital was one of the most memorable of my life. I had a house full of well-wishing friends and family, bringing food, gifts for the new arrival, and tons of interesting information on all things babies. My mother and friends spent the day before we came home cleaning every surface in the house and eradicating all the tick carcasses. And as awful as it sounds, all I could think the whole time the well-wishers were there was, *Go home. I am exhausted. I need rest so I can get my life back to normal.*

Finally everyone left and it was just me, my mother, and my new baby sleeping soundly in his grandma's arms. My mother got up and gave this sweet little sleeping child to me, gave me a hug, and walked out the front door of my house. The door closed with a tight little snap. To me it sounded like a sonic boom went off. There wasn't a sound in the house—no TV, no radio, no dog, nothing. Just stone cold silence. I just stood there in the foyer staring at the closed front door wondering what in the world I was supposed to do now.

It was this exact moment in time that I realized I was not the smartest person in the world. I had clearly gotten myself into a situation that I was wholly unqualified for. The full knowledge of my inadequacy flooded over me as my face flushed and I broke out in a light, misty sweat. I wanted to know what crazy person at the hospital looked at me and thought sending this helpless little creature home with me was a good idea. What about all the well-wishers from a few minutes ago—did they not see that I had none of the necessary skills to be responsible for another human life! And worst of all, what was my mother thinking just sashaying out the door like it was another day in the neighborhood. Things had changed drastically and we clearly were not in Kansas anymore.

Up until the door closed with its quiet sonic boom, I had thought that having a baby was just a natural progression into adulthood. You grew up, got married, and had a baby. Easy as pie. What I had failed to comprehend was the overwhelming responsibility of being entrusted with a small human life. This was nothing like getting a puppy from in front of the supermarket. If the dog doesn't learn to toilet outside, chew only his toys, and bark only when spoken to, you can just give the dog to someone else. Perfectly acceptable— let someone else have a run at it. You can't do this with your child. The birth certificate ties this entity to you. It's like a legal document: You birth it, you raise it.

I had thought raising a child was about bottles and burping, diapers and bath time. Looking at the innocent face of the newborn in my arms, I realized there was so much more. Everything this child will grow up to be, from the idealistic (his dreams and aspirations, value systems, work ethic, behavior public and private, his internal moral compass) to the rudimentary (proper oral hygiene, table manners, when to pick his nose and when not to, not to scratch his private areas in public, no spitting unless you've swallowed a bug)—it was up to me to make sure he learned all of these lessons. All his ideals were mine to nurture. There is a dark side to this equation as well. All his fears, phobias, and neurotic tendencies would be the result of errors in my parental judgment. Everyone knows if you don't potty train properly, your child could end up being one of those kids who sits on the sidewalk pulling the legs off June bugs.

I sat down on the couch and put the baby on my thighs. I brushed my index finger gently against his little check and made my first parental proclamation: *Like it or not, it's just you and me kid. You didn't show up with an owner's manual and I have no idea what I am doing, but we'll make it through together.*

Then he started to cry.

In retrospect, I think one of the reasons I decided to have a child at a young age was that I wanted someone who would love me always and forever. I thought having a child would create the unconditional love I craved so desperately. What I found out was that I was the one giving the unconditional love. Children want what they want when they want it, without regard to whether it is appropriate or not. This attitude, by definition, means that as a parent, you can be adored one second and loathed the next. Raising a child is a test of endurance, will, and truly a labor of love. But I know the most important thing I have done with my life is raise my children. They are my true shining stars and I will always treasure every experience of their growing up.

Chapter 2

A World of Firsts

All Moms Cry in the Shower

By Kae

The days after my son was born went by in a blur of bottles, diapers, baths, and crying. Lots and lots of crying. I lived in a brand new 1980s ranch house where the master bedroom was on one side of the house and the other two bedrooms were on the other side. Before my son's birth I had read a myriad of *All the Goofy Advice About Babydom* books so that I, too, could be the best mother in the universe. In reading these tomes, I realized I was a failure from the get-go because nursing was not going to be an option for me. I was going to be a single mom. I had to go back to work as soon as possible after the blessed event. Strike one. I was also going to have to put my child into daycare. Strike two. I was already down in the count before I'd even birthed the baby.

I should have realized I was woefully unprepared to be a mother when I didn't know what most of the gifts at my baby shower were for. I'm sure there are still some of these items boxed up in my attic. I never did figure out what they were for, but just the same, I was afraid to get rid of them.

There were concepts I read about that I just didn't understand— like swaddling. Why in the world would you wrap a child tightly in a blanket? This made no sense to me. I didn't think it was a way for the baby to feel more secure. We are talking about the same baby who has been floating around buck-naked for the last nine months. I thought under those circumstances being swaddled would feel more like being bound and gagged. Wrap the baby nice and tight in the blanket and then shove a pacifier in his mouth and just hope his nose is not stuffed up. No.

But the *All the Goofy Advice About Babydom* books said that good mothers swaddled, so I swaddled. Good mothers fed their newborn babies four ounces of formula per feeding, so I fed exactly four ounces. Good mothers rocked while feeding, so I rocked. Good mothers bathed their baby regularly, so I bathed. Good mothers changed diapers regularly, so I changed. Good mothers used diaper rash cream at every diaper change, so I slathered my son's young rump in diaper rash cream even though there was no sign of a rash. Children of good mothers were content and therefore did not cry.

Matthew cried and cried and cried.

I was taken aback by my son's response to me. I had spent at least six months talking to this baby through my ever-growing belly about how life was going to be. I sang to him. I ate for him. Heck, I gave up beer for the buzzard. I had watched all kinds of movies, sporting events, and competitions where the person in the spotlight mouthed "Hi Mom" or otherwise glorified the relationship between mother and child. I had stressed to this child in the womb how it was just the two of us, and proclaimed it again on his first day in our home. I had waited for long months of bloated agony to birth the child who was going to fulfill my need for unconditional love. To my surprise, the kid hated me. I was a failure according to the *All the Goofy Advice about Babydom* books, and I had just grazed the tip of the iceberg of Motherdom.

The books said not to let the baby sleep in the room with you, but Matthew's nursery was all the way on the other side of the house. When I was preparing for the blessed event, I never would have thought the placement of his nursery could cause me so much distress. I checked several of the *All the Goofy Advice About Babydom* books and sure enough, it was a consensus: Don't put the baby's crib in your bedroom. Once again, this was advice that made no sense to me at all. I have carried this baby in my body for the past nine months. We have literally spent every single moment together for the last 270 days and nights. Now the various "experts" decree it's important that we don't share the same space—but to make sure the child is secure, wrap him tightly in a blanket. This was nuts!

Every mother becomes paranoid at one time or another. Early in my children's lives, my nemesis was sudden infant death syndrome—SIDS. I was convinced that if I could not hear them breathing, they would cease to do so. There was no way I was going to put this new baby all the way across the house and tempt the fate of SIDS. Also, what would happen if I fell asleep and he started to cry and I didn't hear him right away? Would this constitute strike three? Would he be scarred for life at the tender age of three days?

After much deliberation and research, I decided the solution was to put the portable crib right outside my bedroom door. Technically, the baby was in the other room (the hallway) while, in terms of proximity, he was about three feet away from my head as I slept.

As is customary with newborn babies, I was up with Matthew every two hours and sometimes less. The only time Matthew slept longer than two hours was in the middle of the day. Sometimes he would go for three then. At each feeding I would give him exactly four ounces of formula, rocking diligently back and forth, then change his diaper and slather his tender buttocks with diaper rash cream before putting him back to bed for an hour or so.

On day six, I earned strike three. Waking up at four a.m. for the fourth time in seven hours, I prepared the requisite four-ounce bottle and sat in the kitchen chair for the obligatory rocking and feeding. I was exhausted. I hadn't had more than two hours of sleep since the baby was born, not to mention the fact that one of the reasons I wanted things to get back to "normal" before I had him was that I was not sleeping well.

So there I was, before the crack of dawn, not a bird to be heard, sitting at my kitchen table with my newborn baby boy cradled delicately in the crook of my arm. I put the nipple of the bottle into his mouth and watched lovingly as he began to suckle the formula from his artificial mom. Looking at his amazing little blue eyes, I began rocking gently to and fro, to and fro, and then I drifted back to sleep.

I woke up with a start, some never-to-be-determined time later, to find my sweet little boy with his head and shoulders hooked in the crook of my arm but the rest of his little body dangling down beside the chair so that his feet almost touch the floor. I was mortified. I looked down into his little face, with his amazingly blue eyes, still sucking greedily on his bottle—which, for the record, I had not dropped or dislodged from his mouth. I pulled him back into my lap and told him we would speak of this to no one. Since he didn't argue with me, I assumed he was in agreement.

The day went by in an exhausting flurry. When I changed his diaper at noon I noticed that there were little red blisters on his bottom. I took extra care to slather a thick layer of diaper rash cream on his bottom. He had begun to have loose stools and I thought maybe the culprit was the stomach acid in the diarrhea. The next feeding went fine, but afterward the crying began. He drew his knees up to his chest, his face reddened, and he basically screamed bloody murder for the next hour and a half. The next feeding went the same, except he never quit crying. I had fed, diapered, and creamed him, and still he cried. I swaddled, he cried. I rocked, he cried. I paced, he cried. I sang cute little baby songs, he cried.

My friend and current roommate, Cindy, came home after work. I had not had a shower in days—a fact Cindy did not neglect to mention that she noticed. My precious little bundle of joy was still crying when she came in.

"Go take a shower and get some clean clothes on. I'll take care of the baby until you get done," she said as she took the wailing bundle of joy from my arms.

This child who had been crying since noon instantly fell silent in a virtual stranger's arms. I had done everything that the *Idiot's Guide to Babies* had said good mothers did and still my child was in distress. Then this person who didn't even have children and who had never read the myriad *All the Goofy Advice About Babydom* books walked in and suddenly Mr. Cries-a-Lot became silent as a lamb.

I went to the shower and turned the water on as hot as I could stand it. I washed my straggly blonde hair, washed my over-ripe body twice, shaved the mat of hair from under my arms, and shaved the three inches of growth from my legs. Then I sat on the floor of the shower and cried my heart out. After only six days, I had completely failed as a mother. In one day I had managed to hang my child from his neck during a feeding, he was clearly infected with some kind of baby dysentery, he had a blooming case of diaper rash, and he was more content with a virtual stranger than with his own mother. Motherhood was going to be much more difficult than my rose-colored glasses had anticipated. I was overwhelmed with hormones, sleep deprivation, and maternal responsibility.

I would like to say this was the one and only time I took to the shower for a good whine and cheese party, but that would be misleading. Over the next 24 years, I took to my shower on more occasions than I can count. Thankfully, I came out refreshed both physically and mentally each time.

Many months and several showers later, I found out that Matthew was allergic to milk. He was also allergic to the batting in the diapers I was using and, just for a kicker, he was allergic to the diaper rash cream that I had so diligently applied to his tender and reddening buttocks. He also did not like to be cuddled too long or wrapped too tightly in either blankets or binding clothing. He was sensitive to fabrics that were "scratchy." He also had a brilliant appetite. Once the formula was straightened out and I started feeding him oatmeal, he was happy as a clam and would go sometimes as many as six hours before becoming ravenous and demanding an eight-ounce bottle of soy-based formula and his bowl of oatmeal.

I kept the *All the Goofy Advice About Babydom* books on the shelf in my living room. I still looked at them from time to time, but I realized something so important that day sitting on the floor of my shower feeling sorry for myself: It didn't matter if I had just earned strike three or if my son was more content in the arms of a stranger than in mine; I was stuck with him. He did not come with a refund or an exchange receipt. And either unfortunately for him or fortunately, depending on the date and time, neither did I. I was his mother and he was my child. I knew that I would have to find my own way and my own style as a mother. The books were all great for reference, but this was a new adventure and I would have to forge my own path. My journey into motherhood had just begun.

Yikes, I'm a Mother

By Pam

We arrived home from Guatemala with Gracie on a Wednesday evening. Waiting for us were my in-laws and my mother. I was exhausted but elated. When I finally put Gracie to sleep in the crib that had been waiting for her for weeks, I was ready for everyone to go home so I could shower, unpack, and then go back into Gracie's room to simply stare at my beautiful sleeping child.

When the last of our family left and we closed and locked the front door, Scott and I tiptoed back to Gracie's room and peered in. *We were parents!* Our child was safely in our home. All the months of waiting, worrying, and nailbiting were over. We were a family. We stood in the doorway of Gracie's room and embraced each other. It was more intimate and loving than any other time we had ever held each other. It was an embrace that said we were no longer just a couple—we were Gracie's parents.

After several moments in this quiet, intimate, and heavenly embrace, I felt my body doing less embracing and more leaning. Although my heart was full, my body was exhausted and the stress of the past three days was reminding me that I'd better get some sleep. Reluctantly, we quietly backed out of Gracie's room and headed to bed.

The next morning, Scott had to go back to work. He had several construction crews on different sites and he needed to check on all of them. Even though I wanted our world to center around our new baby, I knew Scott had to get to work. He asked me if I thought I could handle things by myself, and I assured him I could. If I had handled the past three days in a foreign country with a new baby who had immediately hated the very sight of me, I figured I would do just fine in my own home. I was more than ready to start being a mommy.

Scott waited until Gracie woke up so he could kiss her goodbye before leaving for work. I stood at the front door with Gracie in my arms and watched him until he was out of sight. He drove very slowly in an effort to savor the moment as long as possible.

"Well, let's get started with our day, shall we?" I said as I kissed her on the cheek.

With that, Gracie and I began our first official day at home together. Things that would later become ordinary routines, such as feeding, bathing, brushing hair, picking out what to wear, and playing, were, at this moment, monumental events that I had waited forever to experience.

I put Gracie in her baby swing so I could prepare a bottle for her. As I buckled her seat belt and turned the switch on the swing, I felt a wave of peace and contentment flow over me. I was looking into the eyes of my beautiful daughter. God had given me the most precious gift and was entrusting me with this baby...what was God thinking? *I'm in over my head! I don't know what I'm doing. Who signed off on this and felt I was mother material? Clearly, someone made a dreadful mistake.*

Suddenly, that wonderful wave of peace was turning into a wave of doubt. *What if I don't have any maternal instincts? I've been childless for so long, am I really able to be as unselfish as a mother should be? I'm not qualified for this.*

I made Gracie's bottle and then removed her from the swing. I sat down in the chair and held her in my arms as she happily drank. I kissed her on the forehead and something happened—something that had not happened since we'd met in Guatemala three and a half days ago: *she laughed*. It was as if she was telling me to stop worrying and that we would get through this together. She also couldn't take her eyes off me. We just sat there together, looking and smiling at each other. I didn't want the moment to end. Maybe we'd be okay after all.

"Welcome home," I whispered.

I had an appointment with the pediatrician that afternoon. The adoption agency stressed that children should see the pediatrician the day after returning home from Guatemala. Even though I wished we could've waited a couple of days before putting Gracie (and me) through that experience, I didn't want to take a chance. So I packed the diaper bag and placed Gracie in her car seat for our first ride to the pediatrician.

I have always been a careful driver, but with Gracie in the car I suddenly became the star pupil of the driver's ed class. To probably every other nearby driver's dismay, I kept by-the-book car lengths between me and any car in front of me. I eased on my brakes when approaching a stoplight so I wouldn't cause my daughter the tiniest bit of discomfort, and when the lights turned green, I smoothly went through intersections in the way my father had spent end-less hours trying to teach me when I was 16. As I thought about mothers in other cars I had seen through the years—talking on the phone, yelling at the kids, passing drinks and snacks to toddlers in the back seat—I knew I would never multitask that way in a car. I would concentrate on the road ahead of me and be the safest driver I could be.

Rest assured, my dream bubble popped rather quickly. I soon became a multitasking mother at the wheel who could compete with the best of them. But on this first day of driving Gracie, I was a shining example of how Tennesseans should behave on the road.

We arrived at the doctor's office and sat in the waiting room with all the other mothers and children. I was so happy. I was one of them. I was in the waiting room of the pediatrician's office. I hadn't been in one of these since I was a child. And now here we were, a mother and her child, sitting in a room filled with other mothers and their...*sick children!* Yikes! I realized that in addition to the cooing of the mothers and the adorable voices of the chil-dren, I was hearing coughing, sneezing, sniffling, nose blowing, dry heaving, moaning, crying, and whining. There were germs lurking all around my precious new daughter. I held her against me and glared at any child who even looked as if he was going to breathe in our direction.

Once in the doctor's office, Gracie was weighed, measured, and carefully examined. I was nervous about how she would handle this first experience, but so far she was calm and relaxed. Her mother, of course, was a different story. Our new doctor was telling me that my baby daughter looked as if she was in perfect health. Then he said that Gracie should have a full blood work-up, just to be sure.

Okay, here's the thing: I certainly wanted to know that Gracie didn't have any underlying health issues. I was even realistic about the fact that she might end up getting pricked with a needle or have some sort of diagnostic testing. I just wasn't prepared for the role I would have to play in this.

We were sent to the lab, where the technician nonchalantly explained the procedure to me. Apparently, someone somewhere came up with the idea that the most helpful role of the mother is to lay her body across the child and look her in the eyes to comfort her as the technician puts the tourniquet on, sticks the needle in, and collects what seems like four quarts of blood. The reason for this, as it was explained to me, is to let the child know that the mother is right there so the child can trust what's going on.

That might have worked in other cases where mothers had already had some quality time with their babies, but Gracie and I had only known each other for three and a half days, and most of those days were spent with Gracie hating the very sight of me. Now I was going to place my face right against hers while total strangers stuck a needle in her arm. Our bonding process was certainly going to have some major setbacks after this. And, with my newfound appreciation for how loud and long an unhappy baby can scream, I knew my hearing was going to suffer a setback as well if I placed my head just inches from hers.

When I was a veterinary technician, I always allowed pet owners to leave the room during painful procedures so the animals wouldn't associate them with the experience. I never wanted them to be the bad guys in the eyes of their precious pets. Yet here I was, about to be the ultimate bad guy.

"Whatever you do, don't cry," warned the technician.

"Okay, sure," I responded as tears started stinging my eyes.

Then I did the impossible. I leaned in close to Gracie, gently pressed my body against her, and looked her straight in her beautiful brown eyes with the most calming, comforting look I could muster. And she did what any baby would do in that situation—she screamed her head off right in my ears.

When the technician was finished and Gracie's arm received a bandage, we were free to leave. I quickly carried my screaming, red-faced child through the hallway, through the germ-filled waiting room, and out the front door. I saw a bench just outside the main entrance and sat down with Gracie. I held her in my arms and rubbed her back until she stopped crying, and until I stopped crying as well.

Gracie stopped wailing and was just whimpering at this point. I still held her to me and rocked gently back and forth. I started singing. I didn't want to put her in the car until she was calm. So I did what my newly hatched material instincts directed me to do—I rocked her and sang.

"You're a good mother," an older woman said to me as she walked by us.

I wanted to hug that woman.

I'm a good mother!

The Giggle

By Kae

Frankly, I never really gave the subject of childproofing my house a great deal of thought. I did put plastic electric outlet plugs in all the electrical outlets, but that was about it. So many things just seemed like common sense to me. If you don't want your child to be able to get into something, don't put it in a place where he can get to it. Seems simple enough. I never spent money on cabinet latches. I never put locks on the cupboards or dresser drawers. I never even heard of a toilet lock.

I didn't keep cleaning agents in the cabinet under the sink; these were in the cabinet above the sink where no one who didn't know not to drink them could reach them. Since I had a limited "medicine cabinet," the scant few medicinal items were kept in the kitchen cabinets on the top shelf where the kids could not reach them.

The bottom cabinets in my kitchen never held any item that I didn't want my kids to be able to touch. They were full of Tupperware with mismatched covers and huge aluminum pots with lids that I used to make vats of spaghetti sauce from scratch. On rainy or cold days, the kids would all pick a cabinet and we would make a marching band out of its contents and march around the kitchen table. Christina was always making cymbals out of the lids to the large pots and Matthew loved to make drums out of my salad keeper and wooden spoons.

One significant event changed forever how I felt about child-proofing. Matthew was about a year old and was navigating around our apartment with ease. This was back in 1984, when cordless phones were just a gleam in someone's eyes. When the phone rang in our house, we had to get off the sofa and walk to the wall-mounted telephone in our kitchen. I had attached to the receiver the longest cord you could buy, so that I could reach the entire kitchen and almost to the hallway while still talking on the phone.

Our apartment was configured so that we had a long kitchen across the back of the house that opened out to the backyard. The kitchen flowed through to our dining room. Off the dining room was a small bathroom and a hallway that led to two bedrooms and ended in our living room.

One afternoon, the telephone rang and Matthew and I made the trek from the living room into the kitchen. I always kept a stash of Matthew's toys in the kitchen for when I wanted to talk on the phone. I put Matthew down on the kitchen floor and surrounded him with his kitchen toys.

One great thing about being in my 20s was that I was the queen of multitasking. I would talk on the phone, start the preparations for dinner, make out a grocery list, and play with Matthew all at the same time. This particular day, I was talking to my mother-in-law, getting a chicken with potatoes into the oven to roast, and making out a grocery list. I stepped into the pantry to see what we needed in the way of dry goods. When I returned, literally no more than a minute had elapsed; Matthew was nowhere to be seen. For most parents, it's probably a common occurrence to turn your back and find your toddler has toddled away. For me, this was very rare. Matthew was the type of child who would sit and play with a car or a ball for hours and never leave the area. Matthew was not an adventurer or a wanderer by nature.

Continuing to keep up my end of the pleasant banter with my mother-in-law, I went to the opening into the dining room. A quick survey of the room made it clear that Matthew was not in the dining room. I squatted down so I could look under the table and chairs. Maybe he was playing hide-n-seek. No Matthew. I stretched the phone cord as far as it would stretch so I could look around the room and down the narrow hallway to the living room. No Matthew.

Then I heard "the giggle." You know the giggle—the one the parent of a toddler quickly learns means, "I am into something and it will be a great big burly mess for mom to clean up." Yep, I heard that giggle. The giggle was coming from the small bathroom that was just off the dining room.

The odd thing was, I almost always kept the bathroom door shut. I kept the door shut so Matthew couldn't venture in and pull all the toilet paper off the roll before I caught him. I also kept the bathroom door shut because it opened directly onto our dining room about where the hallway to the front of the house was. To get from front to back in the house you had to pass the bathroom door. I kept the door closed because I felt it was unsightly to be staring at our blue toilet every time we walked past.

"Mom, I have to go. Matthew's into something I need to take care of." I hung up the phone and rushed toward the bathroom.

Furiously, my mind was racing through all the things in the bathroom that could elicit "the giggle" from Matthew. I never kept anything under the sink except a plunger and a few extra rolls of toilet paper. I didn't think that toilet papering himself would elicit "the giggle."

There was nothing in or around the sink that could be a problem, since our toothbrushes and razors were kept in the medicine cabinet (which technically held no medicine at all) above the sink. On the far side of the bathtub was a bottle of shampoo and a bar of soap. Surely Matthew, who was barely moving around on his own, had not yet figured out how to climb into the bathtub to get at these items. This left nothing in my mind except, "Did you put the toilet seat down the last time you used the bathroom?"

Relief washed over me like a wave. If Matthew was playing in the toilet water, at least I was fairly sure I had flushed the last time I was in there. Since becoming a stay-at-home mom, I had cleaned the porcelain off the bathroom fixtures. I was not overly concerned about the germs. One thing I had learned not to be was a germophobe.

Just after Matthew was born and while I was still in the "sterilize the world" mode, my grandmother had taken me aside at a family function. "You know, Kae, everyone will eat a pound of dirt before they die." I understood her point and took the "sterilize the world" down to a more reasonable level. I continued to worry about rinsing pacifiers and the fact that Matthew sucked his thumb even though he had just finished playing on the public park swings. The final straw in my attempt at the sterilized world was the day I found Matthew with the wings of a fly sticking out of his mouth. Fine, grandmothers are always right. If a person is destined to eat a pound of dirt before they die, Matthew was getting a head start.

Although I may have been okay with the germs in our house, I was briefly concerned about Matthew having his head near a body of water. What if he pulled himself up on the edge of the toilet to play in the water and somehow slipped in? Is the hole around the toilet seat actually big enough for him to fall in or would he just hit his eye on the side and sport a shiner for a week? Would he have the strength to get himself out or would he drown himself? Luckily for me, since he was giggling "the giggle," I knew his head was well above the water line.

I went to the door of the bathroom and peered quietly in so I could see what was amusing Matthew so. To my horror, he was finger painting on the outside of the bathtub with his own blood! Next to him on the floor was the overturned wastebasket. I suddenly remembered getting out of the shower that morning and throwing away a disposable razor in the trash after shaving my legs. Matthew had gone dumpster diving and had come up with the discarded razor in the trashcan that generally held nothing more dangerous that a bugger-filled Kleenex.

I grabbed Matthew up and ran cold water over his bleeding finger. There were two small cuts on the end of his pointer finger. Luckily, it was a disposable safety razor and not an old-fashioned double-edged razor blade. I was mortified. How could someone with a toddler be so irresponsible? I felt horribly guilty. I had not only carelessly thrown away an object that could injure my child, but I had also carelessly left the bathroom door open so that he had easy access.

Looking back, I realize that this experience made me a better mother. Matthew had never wandered from my sight before. I had been lulled into a false sense of parental security. I had believed I was the one in control—that somehow, my skills as a parent had conveyed to Matthew that he was to stay in my sight at all times and not touch things that didn't belong to him. The reality of childproofing is this: You must be in your child's sight at all times. Childproofing my house didn't mean putting locks on cabinets and latches on doors. It meant paying attention to my child, knowing where he was at all times, and making sure that I didn't inadvertently put anything harmful within his reach. Childproofing meant taking responsibility for providing a safe environment for my child. It was my responsibility to teach him what to touch and what to leave alone.

Pod Gracie

By Pam

Gracie was not an easy baby. She had major separation issues when we first brought her home from Guatemala. She had lived with a foster mother for four months and then suddenly she was in the arms of a total stranger. I also found out from her foster mother that she used to put Gracie to sleep by placing her on her chest while they rocked in the rocking chair. Apparently, the foster mother would sit that way for most of the night. I have a bad back and I spent a great deal of money on a bed that would ease my pain. Spending the night in a rocking chair was out of the question unless I was willing to never walk upright again. So imagine Gracie's extreme displeasure when she realized she was going to have to sleep in a crib.

Once Gracie got over her initial total panic at the very sight of me, she switched gears completely and decided I was the only human being who could hold or touch her. Life went smoothly for her as long as she was somehow physically connected to me.

She would happily let me hold her, but if another human was present and moved a bit too close, she'd scream and cling to me. She'd happily accept a toy offered by me, but should anyone else dare to present a toy or a gift, the vocal siren button was hit and peace would instantly be shattered.

After a couple of months, Gracie's behavior morphed into something more unpredictable. If she was in the mood, she would gladly allow someone to hold her or interact. There was no warning beforehand though. Guests in the home interacted with Gracie at their own risk. You just never knew what you were going to get when you socialized with my daughter. Friends and family were hesitant about holding their arms out to her for fear of having them practically bitten off. Yup, Gracie was moody. People who came over to the house learned that it was always best to ask what kind of mood Gracie was in before they attempted to go near her. She was like a little Yorkshire Terrier who looked so cute and adorable, only to end up being a fur-covered piranha.

When Gracie was in a good mood, we began to refer to her as Pod Gracie—a reference to the old science fiction movie *Invasion of the Body Snatchers*. If I was holding her and Scott came in the room and wanted to hold her, he'd first ask me if it was Gracie or Pod Gracie. If it was Pod Gracie, then he had a green light to cuddle, tickle, and hold her. If it was Gracie, then he waved at her and kept his distance.

If I had to go grocery shopping, it was crucial to time it for when Pod Gracie was in attendance. Shopping with Pod Gracie was fun as we giggled and zigzagged up and down the aisles. I could get all my shopping done in a calm, efficient way. Shopping with Gracie, however, meant getting only the absolute necessities to sustain life and trying to prevent strangers from making eye contact with her.

Gracie was born with a beautiful head of thick, dark hair. It has only gotten more beautiful as she's grown. From the day we brought her home, people have remarked about her incredible hair. She's also a beautiful girl with gorgeous, expressive, dark eyes. Shopping with her always means at least one person will come up to me and tell me how beautiful my daughter is or what lovely hair she has. When I would shop with Pod Gracie, it was no problem having strangers come up to compliment her. If it wasn't Pod Gracie, though, they got a dose of Linda Blair in *The Exorcist*.

One day I was standing at the deli counter. I had Gracie in the infant carrier atop the shopping cart. I was waiting for the deli clerk to finish my lunch meat order. Gracie was in rare form and I was being careful to position the shopping cart so she and the deli clerk's eyes wouldn't meet. Out of the corner of my eye I noticed a woman looking at us and smiling. She had one of those smiles women get when they simply can't resist coming over to tell you how cute your child is. I knew that smile all too well. Unfortunately, I accidentally made eye contact with her as she was steering her cart in our direction. If she came over and tried to talk to Gracie, I knew it would set my daughter off screaming and then I'd never be able to finish my shopping. I looked at the woman and gently shook my head, signaling her not to approach. It didn't work. Her cart just kept heading our way.

I watched the clerk wrapping my order for what seemed like hours. Ordinarily I would have appreciated his meticulous attention to accuracy and cleanliness, but right now I just wanted him to toss the turkey in a plastic bag and slap a label on it. Unfortunately, the label was stuck to his plastic-gloved fingers and he was slowly and carefully trying to peel it off intact. I was almost ready to tell the clerk to just keep the glove attached to the label and affix it to the blasted bag when he finally got the two separated and handed the package to me. I spun the cart around and sprinted away from the rapidly approaching smiling woman.

Down the cereal aisle I went, tossing groceries in the cart at a fast pace, not paying attention to what was on sale. Shopping with Gracie was like having a ticking time bomb in the shopping cart.

I was almost done. I just had one more aisle to go down to get coffee for Scott. I turned the corner and almost smacked my cart into...the smiling woman. The time bomb ticked louder. I feared for the ears of innocent shoppers around me.

"Oh, is this your daughter?" she gushed. "I noticed her before. She's so beautiful."

"Thank you," I said as I tried to maneuver my cart past her. Tick... tick...tick...I saw Gracie take a big breath in—the precursor to one heck of an ear-splitting sound. The four wheels on the shopping cart were each trying to go in their own directions, causing the cart to jerk. With Pod Gracie, a jerking shopping cart can be a fun ride. With Gracie, however, a cart with defective wheels became a flame traveling up a short fuse.

"And what a head of hair, she has," the smiling woman said. Tick...tick...tick...She leaned over the cart and smiled at Gracie, but it was too late. The fuse had burned down. We were all toast.

Gracie took one look at her and let the siren rip. "WAAAAAAHHHHHHHH!"

The woman straightened up and backed away from the cart, apologizing. "I'm so sorry," she said, "I didn't mean to upset her."

I watched as a few shoppers who had planned to come down the aisle suddenly backed their carts up. It was not worth hearing loss just to buy a can of coffee.

"It's not your fault," I told her. "You had no way of knowing it wasn't Pod Gracie."

"Pod?" she asked, confused, but I had already spun the cart around and was speeding toward the self-checkout. If Scott wanted coffee, he'd just have to get it himself.

Toe to Toe

By Kae

Keeping the children safe led to some odd behavior on my part. Our first house had two staircases. One paneled wood staircase went down into the living room and one narrow staircase went down into the kitchen. I was petrified that Matthew would fall down the stairs. He had just learned how to walk and was still pretty unsteady on his feet. For the longest time, Matthew and I would crawl up the stairs together, both of us on our hands and knees. We would slide down the stairs side by side on our bottoms. When he became a big brother, he made sure that Christina went up and down the stairs the same way. He didn't want her to fall either.

After your child becomes mobile, it seems like all your decisions are rated on the Child Safety scale. Our first house had an old white brick firebox that the previous owners had used to burn their trash. One of our first renovations on the house was to replace the old firebox with a beautiful red brick and mahogany fireplace that was in keeping with the Victorian architecture.

The demolition was finished and the brick layer had come to lay the new brick. David and I, along with my mother-in-law and father-in-law, were discussing with the brick mason the design of the new surround. His English was broken and our contractor did a lot of interpreting for him. In the course of our conversation, it came up that the brick mason was a former football player for the Chicago Bears.

Everything went along fine until we got to the hearth. "I want you to build up the hearth so it doesn't sit flush with the floor like this one did," I said as I pointed to the existing hearth. I was concerned that this would entice the children to crawl right into the fire like something out of a Brothers Grimm story.

"Good, we raise brick," the brick mason agreed with me in his heavily accented English.

"And I think it should come out to about here." I pointed at a spot I had measured out on the floor with the toe of my shoe. I wanted the hearth to be extra deep so I could sit with the children on the edge of the hearth and not have to worry about our bottoms being too close to the flames.

"Not standard" the brick mason indicated as he swiped his steel-toed, work boot-clad foot over my mark on the floor. "Here standard for hearth." And he drew an imaginary line with the toe of his work boot.

"I know it's not standard, but I want it to be deeper than that. I want it to come out to here," I said as I pointed to my mark on the floor with the pointed toe of my shoe.

In an effort to fill his role as interpreter, our contractor tapped the toe of his work boot on the same spot as the brick mason and said, "This is the width of our standard hearth."

Here I was, a five-foot-tall, 90-pound mom stubbornly pointing the toe of her shoe at a line on the floor while a mountain of human flesh that used to be a football player for the beloved Chicago Bears pointed the toe of his steel-toed work boot at a line much closer to the proposed fireplace.

Luckily for me, my in-laws and David, all came to my rescue by adding the toes of their shoes to my spot on the floor. Our spot won, four toes to two. There is safety in numbers after all.

My next design concept was to angle the corners of the hearth instead of leaving the front corners straight with sharp pointed ends. The fireplace was nestled on a wall between the staircase and the case opening into our dining room. This was the only avenue to get to the kitchen and therefore was going to be a major throughway for my family. The floors were hard wood and I could just see Matthew running around the corner, sliding in his stocking feet, and crashing his tiny face into the sharp edges of the brick fireplace hearth.

The four of us had discussed the design of this fireplace for weeks before the brick mason arrived. We had argued the merits of height, width, and angles of the design until we were in complete agreement. David was especially on board with the hearth being angled at the corners to protect Matthew's tender little face. My mother-in-law was thrilled with the drama the angled corners would create in our living room.

I explained my concept to Mr. Former Football Player while he stood and shook his head back and forth in the "lady you're crazy" way he had seen other contractors use on homeowners who asked for designs that were outside their normal mode of operation.

"No, can't be done," Mr. Former Football Player announced with a shake of his head.

"Sure it can. All you have to do is turn the bricks on the ends so that they make a line like this," I pointed the toe of my shoe and drew out an angle at the edge of the imaginary hearth.

"Bricks no lay like that." Mr. Former Football Player swiped the huge toe of his work boot over my imaginary line. "It must be so," he said as he drew out the distinct corner of our imaginary hearth.

"No, it doesn't," I began to protest.

"We have done hundreds of fireplaces and they all have this type of hearth," the contractor chimed in.

"I don't care how many fireplaces you've done. Just because that's all you've ever done doesn't mean we can't do it a different way."

"If you make like this"—Mr. Former Football Player swiped the toe of his work boot at an angle on our imaginary hearth—"the brick will be too long here," he said as he pointed with his toe to where a full brick on the angled corner would end inside the hearth. "This not possible to do."

"If he says it can't be done, then just do it the regular way," my father-in-law suggested.

"No, I don't want it that way. It will be dangerous for Matthew."

"This is the way hearths are always done. I don't think it will be dangerous for Matthew," my mother-in-law offered. She had gone over to the other side.

"I don't care how they always are done. This isn't rocket science. All we have to do is put the bricks on an angle. It's not that hard."

"Sweetie, maybe we should just do it their way." Just like that, David put his toe in with the other camp. Now it was five toes to one.

"Well, if you don't want sharp corners here in the doorway," our contactor interjected, "then we can just put the hearth flush with the floor and that will solve all the problems."

"That doesn't solve anything," I said, probably in retrospect a bit harshly. Anyone who really knows me understands that I technically have one nerve and this guy was all over it.

David and I had been together long enough that he knew nothing good was about to happen. Running his hands through his hair in a gesture I would learn meant, "It's getting uncomfortable and I will be leaving now," he gathered up Matthew and muttered under his breath something about going outside to play. My in-laws followed David's lead and left the house as well.

Mr. Former Football player told me he had a lot of work to do before he actually got to the part of the hearth we were arguing about. He went back to work and I shadowed him, watching in awe as he took bricks and laid them so precisely. He added brick and mortar and leveled all the way across the front of the fireplace. When he came to the end of the row he was working on, he only needed a part of a brick. He grabbed the brick and went out into the yard. Fascinated, I trailed him outside. I was thinking he would use some kind of special saw to make the necessary cut. Instead, he took a hammer out of his tool belt and turned it toward the claw end. Then the wildest thing I have ever seen happened. He put a full brick in the palm of his hand (does that tell you how big his hands were?), reared back with the hammer, and cracked the brick, lickety-split, just where he wanted it.

"That's the most amazing thing I've ever seen," I said to Mr. Former Football Player. He looked up from his work and beamed a big smile at me.

"Can you make a brick any size you want like that?" The answer was a grunted affirmative. "We can do this, we can really do this," I said as I dragged the huge mountain of a man back into the house. I showed him my idea of how the bricks could be broken and placed in a pattern to make the angle I wanted.

To my total astonishment, this man who had been adamant that there was no way possible to create the angled fireplace hearth I wanted was excitedly telling me in broken English how he could accomplish the task.

Believe it or not, this is the most effort I ever put into child-proofing my home. Sure, I have bought a few baby gates and electric outlet plugs and moved dangerous items onto higher shelves. But true childproofing is going toe to toe with a man whose biceps are the size of your waist to protect your child from possible harm.

Chapter 3

Adding On

Hurricane Jack

By Pam

The year we submitted our paperwork to the adoption agency to get a second child, I was also busily on tour with Friskies cat food as their spokesperson. As our waiting time began to wind down, we were informed by our adoption agency that we'd probably be able to travel to Guatemala in about two weeks to pick up our son. The timing seemed perfect, because I was scheduled to be in Tampa, Florida, the following week with the Friskies tour. That was the last stop on the tour, so Jack would be coming home when I was able to concentrate on being a mommy of two.

I left for Tampa on Wednesday evening. I was scheduled to do media events all day Thursday and Friday and then perform with the Friskies cats at the Tampa Convention Center over the weekend. I'd be home with a week to rest up and tackle the last-minute preparations to get ready for Jack. Then my husband and I would be taking that wild trip again to Guatemala to add to our precious family.

Life is funny. You think you have it all planned out and then everything that can go wrong, does. It began with the hurricane. In 2004 Florida got hit with several very severe hurricanes. In Tampa on Thursday, we were informed that there was a chance the hurricane could head toward us, but there was also a slight chance it could bypass us. If it did come our way, it would hit some time on Saturday or Sunday. We were all nervous and thought the show would be cancelled and we'd be able to head home to safety before the weekend. The official word so far was that we were going to wait and see for now, since no one was sure exactly where the hurricane was going to hit.

All day Friday, I was busy doing television interviews in preparation for the event at the convention center. I was exhausted at the end of the day. When I reached my hotel room, there was an urgent message waiting for me. The adoption agency had called. Things had gone faster than expected and we were supposed to be in Guatemala on Monday morning to get Jack. Yikes!

I called the adoption agency and they confirmed it. I wasn't ready. I was in Tampa. After I got off the phone, I paced around the room, trying to calm myself down. *I can do this,* I thought. *I can do this.* I called Scott and we babbled on the phone at each other, not hearing what the other was saying because we were both still in shock. I had some plans to make if we were going to get to Guatemala in time to get Jack on Monday. I called the Friskies office and asked if I could duck out of the show on Sunday. Of course they understood and arranged for a flight for me on Sunday morning out of Tampa. I then made my flight arrangements for Sunday evening from Nashville to Guatemala. I would have a couple of hours at home to pack. I didn't even want to think about how frantic this was going to be, because I had to get through at least one full day at the Friskies show being professional and calm. I'd save the panic for later.

Then the bottom fell out and panic was suddenly front and center. The hurricane was headed straight for us.

An executive from Friskies called to say the hurricane was expected to hit late Saturday night or early Sunday. All flights in and out of Florida were cancelled from Saturday midmorning on. The executive was worried I wouldn't get out of Florida in time to get to Guatemala, so she was trying to get me a flight that very night. But since the governor had instructed everyone to evacuate, all flights out of Florida were booked. I had no way to get home.

I asked about a rental car. She said she'd get right back to me. When she called back, she had bad news: There were no rental cars left. I started to cry.

You might be wondering why I couldn't just hunker down in Florida, wait out the hurricane, and then leave for Guatemala. With Guatemalan adoptions, things are timed to the day. Once you are given clearance, you pick up your child on Monday, go to the embassy to get the visa on Tuesday, then head back to the United States on Wednesday. You must stay those three days—and no other three days. At least that's how it was when we adopted Gracie and Jack. So if I didn't get to Guatemala on Monday, there's no telling how long I'd have to wait to be scheduled again. I wanted to hold my son in my arms as soon as possible.

The Friskies PR person who was traveling with me made several calls in a desperate attempt to find a rental car. I stood at the hotel room window watching the mass exodus and was tempted to just stand on the entrance ramp of the interstate with a cardboard sign, begging for a ride.

I was jerked back to reality when the PR person said she found a car. At a nearby hotel they had the last rental car available in all of Tampa. I threw my clothes in my suitcase and off we went.

It was 5:30 in the evening when I stood at the rental counter in the hotel. After signing all the papers, I was handed the keys and told my car was out front. I was exhausted from my day of media events, and also from the news that my son was waiting for me and that a hurricane was barreling in my direction.

"You'll have to drive through most of the night until you find a hotel vacancy, you know," said the clerk at the rental counter.

"I can do it," I answered. I hadn't had anything to eat since breakfast, I was tired, stressed, and the last thing I felt capable of was driving through the night. But I was going to get to Guatemala and nothing—not even a hurricane—was going to stop me.

Based on how much traffic there was on the interstate, I decided the safest thing to do was stop at a fast food place, grab some dinner for the road, and drive, drive, drive.

I have never been in an evacuation before, and it was quite a surreal experience to be on an interstate for what seemed like forever, going 20 miles an hour. Everywhere I looked, there were cars. Interstate entrance ramps were at a standstill. I felt as if I was in one of those cheesy disaster movies.

I couldn't use the air conditioning in the car because it was dangerously close to overheating due to the snail's pace at which I was traveling, so I rolled down my windows. Almost everyone else had done the same thing, so people were engaging in conversations from car to car.

As I drove, I saw cars and trucks filled to capacity with precious belongings. Many people were prepared for the fact that they might not have a home to come back to, and I'm sure they had their family photos and other irreplaceable items with them. Others were probably vacationers who had to cut short their vacations to head for safety. I felt very sad for the residents of Florida who were leaving their homes, not knowing if there would be anything left when they returned.

After I crossed the border into Georgia, I started thinking, foolishly, that I'd be able to find a hotel or motel room. As I listened to the radio, I learned that every room outside of the hurricane zone was taken. I kept driving.

The radio announcer began to rattle off names of stores that were allowing people to park in their parking lots for the night. He'd read off the location and exit number and it was always the one I had long since passed. I glanced over at rest areas and they were filled with cars lined up one after another. There was nothing to do but keep driving, even though I was getting extremely tired.

To stay awake, I alternated between the radio talk station giving weather and traffic updates, and a rock station. I don't normally listen to rock music but hoped the music would help keep me awake.

The farther north into Georgia I went, the more optimistic I became that I'd be able to find someplace to sleep. But still, every motel was full. It seemed as if everyone evacuating from Florida was headed in the same direction as me. Were we all going to Nashville?

At some point the drive started getting easier for me and I was no longer so tired. I looked over at the seat next to me and saw all the empty cans of Diet Coke and realized that the caffeine had finally kicked in and my head was buzzing. I don't usually drink soda with caffeine and maybe it took awhile before my body realized what I was doing to it, but when it finally did, I was so awake I felt I could drive to Canada. I no longer worried about finding a place to sleep. Instead, I called Scott on my cell phone and told him I'd be home at around seven Saturday morning; I was driving straight through.

The caffeine and rock music almost got me through the entire 15-hour drive. With only about an hour left to go, my brain and body suddenly realized they were being tricked into staying awake. I started feeling as if I was no longer driving a car but rather, pedaling a bicycle. It took great effort to keep my foot on the accelerator pedal. I just kept thinking about my little boy waiting for me in Guatemala. If women could endure hours and hours of labor pain, I could endure the last hour of this drive home. My eyes were burning from hours of oncoming headlights, my nerves were raw from the caffeine assault, and my intestines were making suspicious rumbling sounds from coming in contact with unfamiliar fast food.

Ten more miles...five more miles...one more mile... ahh, there was my wonderful, cracked driveway with the weeds poking through. That driveway never looked so inviting. I pulled up to the house and literally stumbled out of the car. My legs were so stiff and my back was so sore, I just wanted my bed. I walked in the house and I'm sure I greeted Scott and Gracie, but I have no memory of it. I just remember flopping down on my bed and waking up in time for dinner that night.

The next day, Scott and I left for Guatemala to pick up Jack. The hurricane had hit Tampa. I said a prayer and hoped everyone would be okay.

Our flight to Guatemala was calm. It almost didn't seem real that a short time before I had been in total panic in Tampa. We were now both on a plane, on our way to fulfill our dream of having a little brother for Gracie. As I leaned back in my seat, I closed my eyes and wondered whether anyone had checked the weather forecast for Guatemala City.

Big Mac Attack

By Kae

I married David when Matthew was 18 months old. One of our first monumental marital decisions was the timing of expanding our family. I wanted another baby, but I was also going to college full time and didn't want to have to miss a semester. I planned to finish my education and another child would just have to be timed around that. Therefore, we decided it would be ideal to have a baby over the summer. I would be finished with exams and would have a couple of months after the baby was born before the fall semester started.

When I was attempting to become pregnant with Matthew, there had been several months of holding my breath only to find out that the seed was not planted. With Christina, I had a very small window of opportunity. We started at the earliest possible moment attempting to conceive so that there would be time for the maximum number of reseedings. As life would have it, I got pregnant the first time out of the gate. David and I were married in June and we were officially announcing the upcoming birth of our second child by the end of September. This put the baby due the last week of May. The due date was cutting it close—my classes ended May 23. *Oh well,* I figured, *I'll still have a week to get ready after school was out.*

Looking back at this period of time, I am always amazed at how crazy our life was. We bought our first house and I was enrolled in a private college. We were mortgage payments and college tuition poor. Every penny had to be squeezed into a nickel. Time was as precious as the pennies, too. David was a young attorney in Chicago, trudging through the 60- to 70-hour work weeks associates are required to endure to move up the ladder toward partner. I was carrying a full-time course load at school while attempting to carry a baby to full term, keep up a house, and take care of a two-year-old.

Matthew went to daycare until noon each day. The daycare had two rates—half day and full day. Because money was tight, I scheduled my classes so I started at 8 a.m. and ended at 11:15 a.m. five days a week. This meant I only had to pay for half a day of daycare. The private college I attended was in a suburb about 45 minutes north of the one we lived in.

My days basically went somewhat like this: Get up at 6 a.m. (5:30 if I thought bathing was appropriate for this particular day), get Matthew up, fed, and ready for daycare, where he was dropped off by 7 a.m. Shoot down the road to the college, find a parking space (no easy feat), then run like hell to my first class, where I would inevitably arrive just as the door was closing. At this point I would shift into student mode, listening attentively to whatever subject I was taking at the time. At the sound of the last class bell, I would run like hell to my car (assuming I remembered exactly where I parked it) and drive like a maniac back to the daycare to collect Matthew before the half-day rate expired.

Each day at exactly noon, the director of the preschool would go into each room, clipboard in hand, and check off the names of all the children present in the room. If your child was present, you paid the full day rate—even if you were trying to push past her into the room. If the check mark made it onto the paper, you paid the price. Our last name was Allen. We were the first to be assessed the penalty of one yellow traffic light not run in the interests of the health and wellbeing of other drivers on the road. My frenzied drop-off and pick-up procedure worked perfectly, though, until I started the spring semester.

It was a cold and snowy day. The first class of the day was cancelled, but I kept to my normal schedule because I thought it was best for Matthew to never get the idea that the morning routine was flexible. So I dropped Matthew off at the daycare at exactly 7 a.m. and started driving to school. Since I had extra time, I pulled into the McDonald's that was on the way. I took my books in, got a coffee, and inexplicably heard myself ordering a sausage and egg biscuit. I have never in my life before or after had any desire to put that heart attack on a biscuit in my mouth. The thought of it now as I write this is making me feel vaguely nauseous. I ate my future heart attack, drank black coffee, and studied for my next class. After school, I made the mad dash to daycare and all returned to normal. That is, until the next morning.

I woke with the birds the next morning and somewhere between waddling down the hallway to the bathroom and struggling into my elastic-paneled pants, the thought of the sausage and egg biscuit crept into my mind. It started out as a minor *that would be yummy* thought, but by the time I was gently waking Matthew from slumber, it had become a ravenous need. Whipping Matthew's pajama top off and yanking down his pajama pants, my mind was working out the logistics of procuring the increasingly necessary sausage and egg biscuit.

It was decided. I would race into the parking lot of the daycare center, whip Matthew out of his car seat, and walk (or waddle) as quickly as possible in the door. I would consign my child to the morning staff and haul tail, breaking as many traffic laws as was prudent, so I could to shave a couple of minutes off the trip. I would rush into the drive-thru lane and eat in the car on the way to my marketing class. If I timed it perfectly, I would be only a few minutes late. If questioned by my mild-mannered professor, I would simply tell him that I had to use the restroom. This was a shameless misuse of my condition, but it would just be this one time. Surely I would be forgiven.

And this is how my addiction to sausage and egg biscuits began. For the next three months I could be found breaking the land speed record in a pathetic attempt to get to the McDonald's before class started. In the beginning, I was able to feed my addiction and still get to class on time or just a few minutes late. As my pregnancy progressed and my ability to move my ever-enlarging belly decreased to that of your basic tree sloth, I came in later and later to class. Finally one day the professor caught me coming in the door and in front of the entire class confronted me about my lack of respect for his class and his time.

Mortified, I ran through my lie options: I had to use the bathroom before class, or now that I was extraordinarily rotund I had trouble getting from where I had to park to class. These thoughts rolled through my mind but, addicted or not, I am still a decent person. So there, in front of this class of 18- to-20-year-olds, I confessed my dirty little secret. I told them all about how I rushed my two-year-old child out of a sound sleep, whipping clothes off and on so fast that half the time he didn't even know he was changed. I told them about buying generic canned vegetables and toilet paper to save the money to fund my addiction. I confessed, "Hi, my name is Kae, and I am addicted to McDonald's sausage and egg biscuits." I told them I had tried to pass by the McDonald's one morning when it was too late to stop, but that by the time I got to the next traffic light I was sobbing uncontrollably and had to turn around and go back. I told them that the women who work at McDonald's have my order ready at the window before I even get there because they know I will be there and am always running late for class. I told them how I thought I had the situation under control before my belly became so enlarged that I used it as a shelf to hold the blessed sausage and egg biscuit when I needed two hands on the steering wheel.

The classroom full of kids gawked at me as if I had two heads. Clearly none of them had ever been pregnant before. Most of them probably still lived at home with their parents. I might as well have been speaking in a foreign language. They just didn't get it. I looked from face to face, seeing the same puzzled gazes. Then my professor began to laugh. It turns out his wife was expecting. He had witnessed firsthand the downward spiral of a perfectly rational woman in the throes of a prenatal craving. He understood! His solution was that I could get my egg and sausage biscuit and bring it to class, as long as I brought him a cup of coffee, too.

My next big issue became getting back to the daycare in time to get Matthew before the half-day rate expired. My waddle was increasing and each day the trek from my last class to the car seemed to take longer and longer. We began racking up check marks on the director's sign-in page at an alarming rate. The budget couldn't handle both my egg and sausage biscuits and the added daycare costs. One of the daycare staff, Ms. Edie, babysat for us occasionally, and I told her about my problem. The next time I was late, I rushed into the daycare out of breath, knowing full well I had missed the time and another expensive check mark would be next to Matthew's name on the list. But there was no check mark.

I went into Matthew's classroom and there was no Matthew, either. Ms. Edie "psst" me. She was in the coat closet. I went to the opening of the narrow hallway that served as the kids' coat and cubby closet. There were Matthew's legs sticking out from under a red rain slicker hanging on a hook. Ms. Edie had saved my bacon. She took Matthew into the coat closet and hid him from the director. Matthew's was the last class the director checked before she went upstairs to check the rooms with the four-year-olds. I was saved. And this is how we avoided having to pay the full day rates in daycare for the next couple of months. Ms. Edie to the rescue!

The remainder of the semester went on with my marketing teacher and me having our symbiotic relationship and my sausage and egg biscuit addiction somewhat under control. I grew ever larger and began to gain some notoriety among my classmates, who were amazed I was still attending classes right into my ninth month.

My pregnancy was uneventful until the beginning of the eighth month, when I inexplicably gained 24 pounds in three weeks. Ruling out toxemia and diabetes, it was put down to "unknown" and life went on—except now I had to be weighed every week along with the lovely "exam." For two weeks all was fine, and then the doctor informed me that I had dilated to two centimeters. Although I wasn't having any prelabor symptoms, the blessed event was rapidly approaching.

I gave birth to Matthew in four hours start to finish, so the doctor forbade me to be more than 20 minutes from the hospital at any time. This created a major issue for me. I had two weeks left in the semester. I was going to be taking finals the second of those two weeks. There was no way I was going to miss the last two weeks of school, miss my finals, and then have to go back later in the summer and take them when I had a two-and-a-half-year-old and a newborn to contend with. The school was about an hour from the hospital. I decided to go for it. Worst case scenario, I would go into labor at school and have to get someone to drive me to our hospital ASAP.

I talked to my friends at school and we set up a plan so that in each of my classes I had a designated driver if I needed one. I talked to my professors and they were all on board. The week of finals came and everyone was on pins and needles. I had dilated to four centimeters but still no contractions and my water did not break. On Friday, I took my first of the day's finals and then went to my French class. I had been taking a class in conversational French and my professor was a wonderfully sweet woman. We were supposed to have a stand-up oral final. My professor took one look at me and sent me home. She said she knew how nervous I got when I had to speak in front of the class and the last thing she wanted to do was deal with me going into labor during her final exam. My final was to write an essay in French about the birth of my baby and send her pictures. That was it. I was done with school!

With a sigh of relief from all my designated drivers, I drove out of the school parking lot and back into the 20-minute safety zone. I picked up Matthew from daycare, then went to the video store and rented *The Amityville Horror*. It was a movie David and I had wanted to see but hadn't had the time. Tonight we would celebrate the end of the semester by putting Matthew to bed early and eating Chinese food while watching a movie!

We lived in an old Victorian house that shuddered if the wind blew too hard. Halfway through the movie we had to turn it off because it was creeping both of us out. Tired from a long day, we both went to bed happy that we could sleep in the next morning. A few hours later I woke up to go pee. This was nothing new; I was nine months pregnant. All I did was pee. An hour later I was up again; okay, this was a little bit odd. An hour later I woke up again. This time I didn't have to pee. I had a pain and it was very familiar to me. Without any further thought, I knew I was in labor and that time was of the essence. I reached over and poked David. "Dave, wake up."

"I am not getting up with you to go to the bathroom because you're scared," my husband mumbled from his sleep.

"No really, get up. I'm in labor." I have never seen David move so quickly. "Go get in the shower while I call your mom to come watch Matthew," I said as we raced around the bedroom getting our hospital stuff together.

My mother-in-law must have broken every speed record known to man getting to our house. We lived only 10 minutes away, but I swear she was coming in my front door as I put the phone back in the cradle. I've often wondered if she had taken to sleeping with her clothes on as the blessed due date approached.

David and I set out on the 20-minute drive to the hospital, did the check-in routine, and were set up in a birthing suite. Less than an hour and half later, we were the proud parents of one Christina Marie Allen. She was crying like a banshee when the nurse handed her to me. I kissed her on the face and made some cooing noises and she stopped crying and just sighed and fell asleep. When the nurse came to get her to finish cleaning her up, she started wailing again. But as soon as they handed her back to me I just snuggled her in my arms and she sighed and fell back asleep. It was wonderful. Finally, a child who seemed to like me!

The first night they asked me if I wanted to keep Christina in the room with me or have her go to the nursery until it was time for her to eat. I decided that with a two-year-old at home, sleep was a prime commodity, so she went to the nursery. The nurse rolled her away down the hall in her bassinet and I instantly fell asleep. Shortly, a very apologetic nurse awakened me. Apparently, Christina had begun to cry as soon as she was wheeled away and there was nothing the nurses could do to calm her. "Frankly, she is disturbing the other babies," the nurse said. Fuzzy with sleep, I reached my hand over the rim of the bassinet and gently patted Christina's back and she fell silent. "That's the damnedest thing I ever saw. She just wanted her mama," said the nurse as she turned and left the room. Christina stayed with me the remainder of our time at the hospital. She loved to be held. She loved to be cuddled, kissed, and cooed to. I was in pure motherly bliss.

With the birth of my second child I was rewarded with a baby who loved me. It was the most wonderful thing in the world to know that it was me, not a virtual stranger, who could quiet my crying child. One touch of my hand and she was instantly calmed. This child was being nursed. This child loved to be swaddled. This child ate, got a diaper change, and fell into blissful baby mode. Most of all, this child wanted me to hold her and love her. By the criteria set out in my *All the Goofy Advice About Babydom* books, I was finally a good mother.

What I didn't know at the time was that this adoration was a double-edged sword. Nothing I had ever read in my parenting books had prepared me for Christina's separation anxiety. Over the next 21 years and counting, this new dimension of child-rearing would put David and me through our paces. One more lesson learned: Be careful what you wish for. You may actually get it.

Big Bug

By Pam

Even though I'd had a harrowing experience getting back to Nashville from Tampa in time to get on a plane for Guatemala, I was emotionally, physically, and mentally prepared to become Jack's mother. Having survived the trip from hell last time with Gracie, I had mentally prepared myself for the fact that Jack would hate the very sight of me and that there would be virtually no sleep. I had gained a vast amount of maturity since my first trip to Guatemala and would not take it personally if Jack screamed in terror at my slightest touch.

I packed better this time, as well. Instead of cute little burp cloths, I brought industrial-strength cloth diapers to sling over my shoulder for however many gallons of vomit might spew upward from the stomach of my precious new son.

I was ready this time. I would be able to handle the separation anxiety Jack would feel, I wouldn't cry this time should he burst forth with ear-shattering screams. And I brought a baseball cap in case my hair once again became the victim of projectile vomiting. Yes, I was ready. I was an experienced mommy of one, so I knew what I was doing alright.

We decided to stay at the same hotel as last time, even though it was old and a bit on the buggy side, because it was right next to the American Embassy. The day after the lawyer, foster mother, and interpreter bring the baby to the adoptive parents, everyone but the foster mother must go to the American Embassy to apply for the baby's visa. The less we had to be in a car without seat belts and baby seats, the better. So it was worth dancing around the ants in the hotel room to take the short stroll to the embassy.

We arrived on Sunday evening and had dinner at the "restaurant" in the hotel. I don't even want to think about trying to identify the unfamiliar-tasting meat in my hamburger. We then spent the rest of the night preparing the room for Jack's arrival. We settled in to get a good night's sleep because I was quite sure there would be no more restful evenings for me.

There was no air-conditioning in this hotel. There were also no screens on the windows. Apparently, there aren't many flying insects, or maybe Guatemalans don't have the concern about flying insects that I do. To avoid suffocating, we had to open the window in our tiny hotel room. I'm very allergic to bee stings, so the thought of opening a window without the protection of a screen can cause an anxiety attack. I didn't have anything to worry about, though, because nothing flew in our windows during our entire stay. It crawled in instead. But more on my visitor later.

Scott was sound asleep on the bed. It was still light outside. I didn't know why Scott felt the need to get such an early start on his sleeping, because if memory served me correctly, the last time we were in Guatemala his sleep pattern remained totally uninterrupted. I was the one who needed the sleep, but I was about to become a mommy for the second time and I was getting anxious.

I turned on the television. I don't speak Spanish so none of the four or five stations held any interest for me. I turned off the television. I rummaged through my suitcase for my book and then made myself comfortable on the bed.

I was only about five or six pages in when I saw a tiny ant walk across the page. Another ant followed and then another one after that. They were very tiny ants and I remembered from my last visit to Guatemala that there had been several ants in our hotel room but they had politely stayed on the floor.

I smacked at the ants with my hand and got out of the bed to check for more. There was a line of little brown ants crawling up the side of the nightstand and onto the bed (which was wedged very close to the stand). I closed my book and smacked at all the ants I could see.

After whacking several dozen ants with my book, I went into the bathroom to wipe the smeared remains of ant carcasses off my book cover. That's when I saw another line of tiny ants marching across the threshold of the bathroom. I went back to the bed to wake up Scott and close the window, although it didn't really make much difference because there was about a quarter-inch gap all around the window—large enough for anything smaller than a bird to squeeze through.

"I'll go down to the front desk and ask the clerk to get some bug spray," said a very sleepy Scott.

"Good idea," I answered as I continued to whack away at the little soldiers on the floor.

While Scott was gone, all that could be heard in our tiny hotel room was the sound of my paperback book slamming against the floor and walls. That's when I saw Big Bug. He was quietly crawling down the wall toward the headboard of the bed. He must've been some kind of beetle, but not any kind I'd ever seen before. He was big and he was a bug—that was all I needed to know in order to want him dead. This bug could've been leash-trained, he was so large. I watched him from across the room as he inched down the wall and then stopped, almost as if he was trying sneak into the bed and under the covers before anyone noticed. He probably thought I was too busy knocking off all the little ants to notice his big ugly self headed where no woman wants a bug to be headed.

I stopped slapping the book against the floor and straightened up. I held my paperback in front of me and walked toward the bed. Big Bug knew he was in danger because he started skittering very fast. It was a race to see whether he'd make it under the covers before my literary weapon came crashing down. Then Big Bug did something that brings out the squealing, screaming, frightened little girl in me: He jumped! I can handle bugs that move in predict-able patterns, like ants marching in a line, but bugs that lull you into thinking you've got the upper hand with your flyswatter, news-paper, or paperback, then jump out at you—those bugs really creep me out.

Big Bug did a leap right at my head and then landed on the semi-white, threadbare bed sheets and disappeared under the blanket.

When Scott returned to the hotel room to inform me that no one had bug spray, he found the bed stripped of all linens and me standing in the middle of the room violently shaking out every sheet and pillowcase. OCD strikes again!

"What happened?" he asked.

"There's a Big Bug in here," I replied.

"Did you get him?"

"No, but he's in here somewhere and I'm going to find him."

Scott helped me make the bed and then he relaxed back down, ready to resume his sleep. As for me, I went on the hunt. I searched every inch of the tiny hotel room. I even searched through our luggage and then zippered everything up to make it harder for Big Bug to stow away in there. I was only going to be bringing one extra passenger home to America with me, and it wasn't going to be Big Bug.

Tired from my work as the bug hunter, I gingerly sat on the chair opposite the bed (only after thoroughly inspecting it first). I placed my paperback book across my lap and scanned the room with my eyes. Perhaps I could fool Big Bug into thinking I was asleep. I realized that if I wanted to kill the immense jumper, I'd have to be very fast.

The room was very quiet. I was almost asleep myself when I heard a very faint tapping sound. I sat up quietly and looked around. There on the floor in front of the bathroom stood Big Bug. He looked at me. I looked at him. Oh, I can't swear that he actually looked right at me, but when I blinked, his antennae twitched in my direction and that was enough for me. I started to raise myself out of the chair and saw immediately that he made a left, inching toward the dresser. I sat back down and he moved away from the dresser. Big Bug was playing with me.

What should I do? I wondered. *Should I go as fast as I can and try to squish him or should I be nonchalant and try to lure him out?*

"Scott?" I whispered. No answer.

"Scott, wake up," I said louder.

"What it is?" he asked in a groggy voice.

"The bug is here."

"Then kill it," he said as he rolled over on his side.

"He's really big," I said.

"Use your shoe," he suggested, and then rolled farther over on his side in an indication that this conversation was over.

My shoe! Of course! I'll just put my shoes on and at some point Big Bug will make the fatal mistake of crossing my path.

I wore my shoes for the rest of the evening, but Big Bug remained hidden. I also slept in my clothes on top of the covers with my book across my chest. The only fatalities during the night occurred when I got up to go to the bathroom and squished another line of ants marching around the room.

The following morning, we were both so excited about the fact that Jack was going to be arriving at our hotel that I didn't even think about Big Bug. I was too busy preparing myself to meet my son for the first time and gearing up for his inevitable fear of me that would immediately follow.

At about noon there was a knock on our door. Scott opened it and there stood our lawyer, the translator, and behind him, the foster mother with our new son. We invited them in and the foster mother immediately handed Jack over to me. Something was wrong. Jack didn't cry. Jack didn't scream. He even smiled. Was it possible this child actually liked me?

We spent the next half hour signing papers and going over instructions from the foster mother (done through the translator). She had brought Jack's formula, cereal, juice, and a couple of bottles. Even though I packed bottles, we had been instructed, just as with Gracie, not to bring formula. We would be supplied with enough from the foster mother to last us until we got home. That way the baby could transition slowly to whatever formula the new parents preferred.

The interpreter explained to me that the foster mother was putting cereal in Jack's formula. I opened the box and took a sniff. It smelled like Froot Loops. The cereal was obviously loaded with sugar. There was no way I was going to feed that to my son. I politely nodded as the interpreter gave me my instructions.

I placed the opened box of cereal on the dresser, along with the other feeding supplies the foster mother gave me. We all talked for a few more minutes and then they left. We were now alone with Jack.

Scott and I sat on the bed with Jack and played. He was a happy baby. He didn't scream once. I thought maybe they gave us the wrong child because surely I was supposed to have another screaming, terrified child. I was sure that at any minute the lawyer would knock on the door with a screaming banshee in his arms, declaring that there had been an awful mistake. The quiet, happy baby belonged to another family. The red-faced human police siren was actually ours. But there was no knock on the door. Scott and I might actually be the parents of a baby who didn't cause hearing loss.

After holding and playing with Jack for quite awhile, it was time to give him his bottle and put him down for a nap. I went over to the dresser to fix his formula. I was unsure about whether to put some of that awful sugary cereal in his bottle to slowly wean him from it, or just go cold turkey. I decided I'd better play it safe and not shock his little system.

As I reached for the cereal box I saw several lines of tiny ants crawling up the dresser and up the side of the box. I swept them off with my hands and picked up the box to look inside and make sure no ants had gotten into it. I peered into the cereal box and lo and behold, staring up at me, covered in a light dusting of sugary flakes, was Big Bug. I had him now. All I had to do was quickly close the box and dispose of Big Bug once and for all. I was fast but he was faster. In a cloud of sugary dust, he leaped out of the box, onto the dresser, and out of sight. Damn, that bug was cagey.

The decision of whether to feed the sugary cereal to Jack was no longer an issue. I was not about to offer my new son some cereal that had Big Bug's footprints on it. He went cold turkey.

Scott, Jack, and I spent the afternoon strolling around the miniscule grounds of the hotel and sitting on the balcony that overlooked the front entrance. The balcony was only a few feet from our hotel room. Jack was quiet, happy, and it seemed as if we had known each other since the day he was born.

While sitting on the balcony taking pictures, I caught a glimpse of something out of the corner of my eye. It was big and dark, and it crawled across the balcony and then darted into a crack in the wall. You may think it was just another one of those bugs, but I know better. It was Big Bug. I was sure I saw a little glittery sugar dust on his shell as he skittered across the cement. He was following me. He was taunting me. This was war!

After dinner at the hotel restaurant, Scott and I took Jack to our room to prepare him for bed. I scanned the room and when I didn't see any sign of Big Bug, I wedged a towel across the bottom of the door. If it had been him on the balcony that afternoon, he'd have to find another way to get back in our room.

Jack was bathed, fed, cuddled, sung to, and placed in the rickety hotel-supplied crib. The next day would be a big one for all of us because we'd be going to the American Embassy to get Jack's visa.

I turned out the lights but was too excited to sleep, so as Scott snored away in the bed, I sat in the chair and stared at my new son by the soft moonlight coming through the window. When I could no longer stay awake, I leaned over, kissed Jack lightly on the cheek, and headed into the bathroom to wash up for bed.

The hotel was amazingly quiet. It was all so different from our first trip to Guatemala. I smiled to myself as I walked into the bathroom, shut the door, and turned on the light. That's when I heard the familiar faint "tap, tap, tap" of tiny legs trying to support the weight of an immense shell. Big Bug was somewhere in the bathroom. I pushed back the shower curtain...no Big Bug. I looked behind the toilet...no Big Bug. I knew he was there, watching me from some hiding place. I was too tired to worry about him. In fact, I was actually starting to get used to him. I brushed my teeth, washed my face, and left the bathroom.

"Goodnight, Big Bug," I whispered as I stretched out on top of the bed.

"What, babe?" Scott mumbled from the other side of the bed.

"Nothing. Just saying goodnight," I replied with a smile.

"Goodnight, my love."

I didn't see Big Bug the next morning as we hurried to get ready for our walk to the American Embassy to apply for Jack's visa. Everything went smoothly at the embassy and we were back at our hotel room by late morning. Scott would have to return with the interpreter later that day to pick up the final visa. I stayed at the hotel with Jack.

When Scott left for the embassy, heavy rain started coming down. Strong lightning and buckets of rain hit nonstop for almost two hours. I sat in the chair, cradling Jack and trying to distract us both from the loud booms of thunder. Jack fell asleep in my arms and I sat there, despite the storm, feeling a tremendous peace come over me. My family was complete. The son I had been dreaming about was in my arms.

A bright flash of lightning caught my eye and I glanced up at the window, which was leaking quite badly. In the rather large gap between the window and the casing sat Big Bug. Something was wrong though. He looked nervous—if it's possible for bugs to look nervous. He was darting in and out of the opening.

"Are you afraid to go out in the rain?" I asked Big Bug. (By now it seemed quite normal to be having a conversation with the large insect.) Big Bug continued to go back and forth. He didn't know what to do. Then, in an instant, he darted outside to the ledge and fell. It was the end of Big Bug.

The next morning we got up early and prepared to check out of the hotel. Our taxi was waiting outside to take us for another one of those wild rides to the Guatemalan airport. I was ready for it this time. I packed several changes of clothes for Jack and stuffed many cloth diapers into my bag. Baby vomit wasn't going to get the best of me this time.

Even though I knew Big Bug had met his demise at the window ledge, I still completely emptied our suitcases, shook everything out, and repacked all items with a watchful eye so as not to bring anything, even one of those tiny ants, back to the United States.

Scott brought the suitcases down to the taxi and I took one last look around the hotel room just to make sure we hadn't left anything behind. I picked Jack up from the crib and walked toward the door. Just before closing it, I noticed something big and black crawling down the wall from the window. It was Big Bug. Yes, I know there were probably thousands of bugs just like that one and chances are it wasn't the same bug, but there was something in his walk that told me it was him.

"Adios, Big Bug," I said as I closed the door behind me, "I'm taking Jack home."

I know he was probably just lifting his legs to walk, but I swear Big Bug waved goodbye.

Chicken Pox Island

By Kae

By the time my third child was born, I had been mothering for five and a half years. I had suffered through the first-baby terrors of inadequacy and lived to tell the tales. The transition from one child to two was interesting, but by then I had two and a half years of baby protocol and procedure under my belt. I had tried and true methodologies firmly in place. Now I was a mother of multiple children, seasoned and well worn.

I had everything ready and waiting the day I came home with Jessica, the new baby; remember, this was not my first rodeo. I had the changing table stocked with diapers, wipes, washcloths, diaper rash cream, thermometer, cotton balls, alcohol, and everything else I could think of that the newborn baby would require. The baby clothes had been washed and put in the appropriate dresser drawers: pajamas on the top, going-out outfits in the middle, and special occasion outfits on the bottom. The layette was washed and the bassinet was put together and in the corner of the master bedroom, waiting for its charge.

The nesting hormone had taken effect. My house was spit-shined. For the first time since the last nesting hormone incident, all the laundry in the house was washed, dried, folded, and put away. The bed sheets were all changed and fresh towels hung in the bathrooms.

I gave birth to my third child at 8:30 in the morning and had my tubes tied that same afternoon. Three children was going to be enough for me. The problem was, babies are the cutest things in the whole world. My favorite age is between birth and two years, and I didn't want to be tempted to make it four when this one passed from the terrible twos into the horrible threes. So I had that possibility cut off—permanently.

The morning after I came home from the hospital, my husband kissed me goodbye at 5:30 a.m. and went to catch the train to work. I would not see him again until some time after eight that night. I woke up two hours later with the baby ready to nurse and the other two kids ready to have breakfast. Gingerly (having just endured a "natural" birth then having my tubes tied in the same day tended to make all parts south of the belly button want to be treated gingerly), I made my way downstairs with all the kids and into the kitchen, started the coffee, poured the cereal and milk, and sat everyone around the kitchen table to start the day.

With Christina, my second child, I had perfected the fine art of nursing a baby while holding the child in the crook of one arm, going about the day's business with the rest of my body. This raised multitasking to a whole new level. When deciding I was going to nurse my second child, I envisioned long periods sitting in the rocking chair watching as the life-giving nutrition flowed from my body to hers. Then reality set in. When you have two children, you never get to have long periods of anything—not sleep, not private bathroom breaks, not bathing, and certainly not feeding the hungry masses. The only long period sitting while nursing came in the middle of the night when everyone else was sound asleep. Unfortunately, these were not the relaxing moments that Hallmark wants you to think they are, but that's another story entirely.

Obviously, I hadn't spent time with the kids in the last couple of days, since I was in the hospital and they could only come for short visits. They were full of stories about spending time with daddy, eating McDonald's, and pushing buttons in the elevator at the hospital. Grandma and grandpa had brought them new toys and they ran off to the family room to find them. It was wonderful to be home with the chaos that was mine.

When they ran back in and showed me their new treasures, I noticed a few tiny little red dots on each of their faces. I could see several more on their necks peeking out from their pajama collars. It was March in Chicago, so mosquitoes did not seem logical. Ever since my horrific experience with the tick invasion, I was careful to eradicate immediately any and all spider webs I saw—garden variety or otherwise—so spider bites didn't seem logical either. Chiggers maybe, but once again I discounted this because it was March in the north. There were no chiggers.

I finished nursing the baby and put her in the Kanga-Rocka-Roo baby seat on the kitchen table. I pulled the other two squirmy kids into my arms and gave them both big hugs and kisses on the neck while I looked at their little red bumps.

"Let me look at your tummies" I said to them, and watched with horror as they pulled up their shirts together, showing twin masses of small red blister-like bumps on their chests.

"Turn around and let me see your backs." Oh, my! They were covered back and front.

I had never seen the chicken pox before. I knew it was something young children got that their parents told nightmare stories about at the preschool functions I was obligated to attend. Even never having seen it before, I knew beyond any hope, it was definitely chicken pox.

I sent the two infected kids to the family room, keeping the new baby in the kitchen with me. I called the pediatrician's office in a panic. First, I needed to know, how do I handle the two kids with the chicken pox, and second, is this dangerous for the new baby? They explained that because the baby was a newborn, she still carried the immunity of her mother. Therefore, if I'd had chicken pox, Jessica would generally not be susceptible to the virus. Also, the fact that I was nursing the baby further reduced her risk.

As for the two who were infected, I was told to keep them as quiet as possible, make them comfortable with calamine lotion, give them Tylenol for the fever that was sure to come, and keep them inside the house and away from other children for at least 10 days. It should pass on its own. If they were still getting new welts after the 10th day, they told me to call back and make an appointment.

This was the advice from the disembodied nurse on the other end of the phone. The same nurse who would then hang up the phone and go about her business just said, "Keep them quiet and inside the house for at least 10 days." A five-year-old and a two-year-old—quiet—inside—10 days—my ears began to ring.

I called my mother-in-law to see if she might be able to come over and help me out with the kids during the quarantine, but she was babysitting for my nephew who was only about a year old and hadn't had the chicken pox yet. No cavalry this time. My mother-in-law did go to the pharmacy and pick up copious amounts of calamine lotion and cotton balls. These she brought to my house and left by the back door, ringing the bell and running back to her car before I could answer.

"Guess what? We are going to play a game," I told the kids as I pushed my family room sofa and table back against the wall and pulled an old blanket out of the linen closet. "This is Chicken Pox Island," I declared as I spread the blanket out on the family room floor. I put the new baby's portable crib against the family room wall where we could all see her. I went to the kitchen and got three of the kids' plastic cereal bowls with the cartoon characters on the bottom that surprise the kids if they eat all their cereal—clean your bowl and there would be Scooby-Doo and his goofy grin.

Holding the blanket by the corners, I flung it into the air. The kids scrambled underneath it as it floated to the ground. "Get out from under there you little ghosties," I said as I flipped the blanket into the air again. "Hurry before it crushes you." The kids scrambled across the floor like little crabs, giggling and rolling around.

With the blanket finally laid flat to the floor, I began the story of Chicken Pox Island. "Two little kids, a brother and his little sister, are traveling in a boat on the big ocean."

"Come on Steenie [Matthew's nickname for Christina], get in the boat." Matthew grabbed Christina by the arm and dragged her onto the sofa. He sat on his knees facing the arm rest and pretending to captain the boat.

"The ocean is really rough and the kids are tossing all around in the boat." Matthew and Christina started swaying back and forth, pretending their boat was on rough seas.

"The seas are so rough that the kids have to toss over their life rafts and jump off the ship." Matthew threw the sofa cushion he was sitting on onto the floor, preparing to abandon ship. "Come on Steenie, get your lifeboat in the water, we have to jump."

The kids jumped off the sofa onto their makeshift life rafts, pretending to be tossed around by the high seas.

"The kids paddle their life rafts across the water to the island in the distance and to safety."

"Get on the island, Steenie," Matt commanded as he led the way to safety. "There are sharks in the water. Don't get in the water, they will eat you up." Matthew and Christina, bouncing on their sofa cushions, slid their way across the hardwood floor to the blanket and crawled to safety, panting from the exertion.

"Mommy on island, sharks bite you," Christina told me as she and Matthew began to set up camp on the island. I got on the blanket and we were all safe from the sharks. Matthew and Christina, mostly Matthew, spun the tale from there. Five-year-olds have wonderfully rich imaginations. By the time it was all finished, we were stranded on Chicken Pox Island. The island was guarded by sharks and we had to wait for daddy to come home from work to scare them away before we could be rescued.

I gave each child a bottle of calamine lotion and a bag of cotton balls. "Off with your shirts, maties," I said in my best pirate imitation. When Matthew was about a year old, I started holding my hand like it was a gun and pointing at his belly. Then I would say in my best gun slinger imitation, "Up with your hands, little buckaroo." This made getting the shirt off the child easier because his hands were in the air and it also distracted him from the fact that we were changing clothes. Early on, I realized goofy games and voices would distract me and the child from the mundane chores of daily child rearing, making the experience fun for everyone.

I pulled out the plastic cereal bowls and let the children pour in their own calamine lotion. This doesn't sound very exciting to the adults of the world, but to those under the age of five, being allowed to have control over a liquid substance is very big stuff. Matthew and Christina knew that this was a special event. Their faces were puckered with concentration as they poured the pink liquid.

"Be careful, Steenie, don't spill it, it comes out fast." Matthew made sure that even if I thought Christina could handle the chore, he was in charge of ensuring she did it correctly.

I showed them how to dip the cotton ball in the calamine lotion. "Now, find a red dot and dab it on it like this." I illustrated the correct application of calamine lotion to a chicken pox on Christina's tummy.

"It's cold," Christina giggled.

"I want to do one," Matthew said as he put on his serious face and dabbed his cotton ball in his bowl of calamine lotion. I thought he would dot his own pox but I was wrong. He reached out and dabbed one on Christina's tummy.

"I do one," Christina said. With a face just as serious as Matthew's, she dipped her cotton ball into the lotion and reached out and dabbed one of Matthew's pox.

"It *is* cold," Matthew giggled.

This is how the dabbing of calamine lotion began—each child dabbing the other's red dots. Seeing that there was not a lot of direction control with the dabbing, I proclaimed the faces off limits to children; this was my job.

"Mommy, why aren't you in your underwear on the island?" Matthew wanted to know.

"Mommy got dots?" Christina asked with earnest searching of my body for red marks.

"There's one," Matthew said with triumph, pointing out a freckle on my arm. And just like that, I was in my underpants and bra sitting on a blanket, being slathered in sloppy dots of calamine lotion up to my neck.

"Can we put dots on the baby?" my son asked me with glee in his eyes.

"Okay, but not on her face." I pulled off the baby's clothes and laid her down on the blanket wearing nothing but her diaper, just like the other kids. They dotted her all up, making sure not to get any on her face or her belly button boo-boo.

When my husband came home from work, he walked into the family room and found his three kids and his wife stripped down to their underwear, lying on a blanket on the family room floor, covered in quarter-size pink dots.

When I had my third child, I was concerned that the other two might feel cheated by this third person taking up part of my time.

I was prepared to make special time for each one to make the transition easier. Fate intervened. I was given the opportunity to spend the next 10 days totally focused on all three of my children. There were no daily expectations. No one would dream of asking a woman attempting to handle two children with chicken pox and a newborn baby to add one more item to her plate. All I had to do was sit in my underwear and play with cotton balls. All the hassles of parenting were gone, in my opinion. With the children getting my undivided attention, there were no tantrums or behavior problems. With their appetites off because they were sick, we all ate when the new baby ate: little tidbits of cheese, one bite of apple, or a spoonful of peanut butter. It was never about having to eat a specific amount.

Naptime was when the baby fell asleep and we all lay still on our makeshift island and eventually drifted off to sleep as well. I intentionally never told the kids that they were sick. I never asked them if they were itchy or checked to see if they had a fever. To this day, neither of the kids remember this as the time they had the chicken pox. They just remember it as the time they got to play Chicken Pox Island and put pink dots on the baby.

The bond between my children has always been special. Other siblings fight among themselves and some eventually grow up to hate one another. My children have had their moments throughout the years, but it's really hard to break the bond of pink calamine lotion dots.

Chapter 4

All Aboard the Potty Train

The Poo Poo Happy Dance

By Pam

B efore motherhood there was logic and there was reasoning. Things made sense and I could rely on my life being practical and, dare I say it, sane. As a mother, I entered into a foreign world. I agonized over the simplest things and was convinced that every wrong decision guaranteed my child's adult years would include being one of America's Most Wanted.

My worries about my abilities as a mother reached a peak when it came time to potty train my first child. That's when I learned that mothers in the process of potty training become all-consumed and obsessed with the process. Nothing in my few years of motherhood had me reading as many books, searching the Internet as much, or continually sharing poo poo progress reports with friends as when I ventured into potty training. If you're reading this and shaking your head in disagreement, please don't let me know. Let me live in blissful ignorance, assuming I wasn't the only one who spent every waking moment obsessed with when, how, and where my daughter peed and pooped.

Jumping off the cliff into potty training makes you realize that you didn't truly appreciate the diaper years. Even though it wasn't fun to change loaded and toxic diapers, there was something comforting about the fact that all the pee and poop, for the most part, was contained in a neat little package. Once you begin potty training, your entire home becomes fair game. Your child's previous meal could end its journey in any number of places. Her backside becomes a loaded gun, ready to launch its missile in whatever direction it happens to be pointing. This is just one of the many shifts of power that occur in the parent-child relationship. Your child realizes that just by the mere threat of the appearance of "number two," mommy will come running like a track star from the far corners of the house.

My first obstacle with potty training Gracie occurred before I even officially began the process. I made the mistake of trying to research the best potty training method and realized there were too many experts with too many opinions. I have a mother, a mother-in-law, and four sisters-in-law. None of them agreed on when and how potty training should occur. Friends were even less helpful, because they all had their own opinions. I also started to realize that there was actually potty training competition among many mothers. How early one's child was potty trained was something to brag about, as if it was an indicator of future scholarship potential. Who knew pee and poop had such intellectual importance!

I started losing sleep days before the designated potty training day. Should I use pull-ups or just let Gracie go cold turkey into underwear? I watched TV commercials where the toddlers wearing pull-ups looked extremely happy as they immediately noticed the first drop of wetness and ran to their potty chairs. The toddlers were so proud of themselves and eager to achieve the ultimate dryness. I wanted Gracie to be that happy toddler. It looked so easy. Oh, how misguided I was!

I should've just stuck the kid in pull-ups, but since I'm a researcher by nature, I couldn't leave well enough alone. I read books by the parenting experts who said pull-ups would cause confusion and delay the process horribly because the child wouldn't feel when she's wet. Okay, so being the good mother that I was, I crossed pull-ups off my list. I didn't want to have the first child in history to go to college without yet being potty trained. On the other hand, do good mothers put their kids in underwear and pretend everything is normal when poop begins to overtake the pants they're wearing and leave buttock-shaped stains on the carpet? I didn't want to take the risk that the wrong potty training method would scar my precious child's psyche for life. So off to the store I went to buy underwear and lots of carpet and upholstery cleaner.

My next dilemma involved the potty itself. Back to the books I went for the ever-contradictory opinions on the perfect potty. Should it be the adult toilet with an attached potty seat or should Gracie have her own designated potty chair? I know this seems simple, but let me tell you, this is the stuff of nightmares. One of my friends told me that her child became terrified of the toilet after hearing it flush. Okay, so maybe Gracie should use a potty chair— but which one? Before becoming a mother, I would never have imagined you could create so many variations on such a simple theme. I stood in the store trying to decide between potties that played music, potties that verbally offered congratulations on a "job well done," and potties that resembled cartoon characters. I wasn't sure if Gracie would rather sit on a potty with a dancing Winnie the Pooh or a smiling Elmo. There were soft seats, hard seats, handles, no handles, splash guards, no splash guards, folding potties, cheap potties, and pricey potties truly worthy of the title *throne*.

I opted for the potty seat that attaches to the adult toilet. I also bought a step stool because the experts advised that children will poop better if they can set their feet firmly on something. I went home and prepared for my first day as Potty Training Mother. Wisely, I chose to start this on a Saturday so Gracie and I could have the whole weekend for her to romp around in her Cinderella underwear.

When your child pees into a diaper, you can easily be deceived as to the actual amount of liquid a tiny toddler can produce. When that same child pees straight into her thin cotton Cinderella underwear, you start thinking in terms of dams bursting or rivers overflowing. I went through my two bottles of carpet cleaner within the first weekend. By Monday, all the furniture was covered in towels and there were sheets spread out over the carpet.

As we started to have some success with peeing in the toilet, I began to feel that potty training would be easier than I'd been led to believe. That dream was shattered before the end of the third day. Gracie announced that she had to poo poo, so off we went to the toilet. She proudly sat on the potty seat and after what seemed like hours (it feels that way when you're perched on the edge of the tub being a potty cheerleader), I heard the triumphant sound of a tiny turd hitting the water. Yay, success! I jumped up and hugged my daughter, removed her from the toilet, and showed her what a glorious job she had done. Then I did the unthinkable: *I flushed the toilet*.

"Noooooooooooo!" screamed Gracie as she grabbed the toilet seat with both hands and looked into the bowl. My immediate response was that she was afraid of the flushing sound, but how could that be? She had never shown this reaction when we flushed after she peed.

"Gracie, what is it?" I asked as I knelt down next to her and put my arms around her shoulders.

"My poo poo. You took my poo poo," she cried.

Those of us who have been performing this normal bodily function for many years have apparently forgotten how attached children can be to anything they view as theirs. Poo poo is no exception. Gracie didn't want to say good-bye to something that belonged to her. For half an hour, Gracie grieved for her lost poo poo. I was to blame, she reminded me. I drowned the poo poo. I was, as Gracie put it, "the Poo Poo Monster."

I decided that the adult toilet held too many poo poo murder memories for my daughter, so I went out and bought a potty chair. The Winnie the Pooh potty chair that had a simulated flush valve seemed perfect. The battery-operated chair (I never would've imagined I needed to stock up on batteries for my child's potty training) made a mock flushing sound and offered a congratulatory "way to go" and "good job." My plan was for Gracie to see her poo poo in the potty so we could spend an adequate amount of time saying good-bye. She could then "flush" and hear the potty praise her for a job well done. Perhaps if we could give the poo poo a proper send-off before the final flushing, Gracie would forgive me and realize that there would always be another poo poo to take the place of the recently departed one.

When Gracie announced that she had to go to the bathroom and it was indeed a poo poo that she had to do, I nervously sat on the edge of the tub and watched my daughter brace herself on the Winnie the Pooh chair. She eyed me suspiciously—after all, she was pooping in the presence of the dreaded Poo Poo Monster. I tried to keep the conversation light as we waited for her to finish. I talked about the fun day we had playing blocks and how beautiful her crayon artwork was. She wasn't buying it. She looked at me stone-faced. I was still in the poo poo dog house.

Finally, she announced she was done and slowly stood up and turned around to make sure what she had produced was, in fact, still in the potty.

"Oh, Gracie, I'm so proud of you," I squealed as I clapped my hands and then patted her on the back.

"Don't touch it," she ordered.

"Of course not," I assured her. "But you know, your poo poo really wants to go join the other poo poos that are already down the toilet. Your poo poo wants to go home."

"My poo poo has a home?" she asked. She was showing weakness. I might just convince her.

"Yes, of course, dear. We put the poo poo in the toilet so it can swim home to be with the other poo poos. What would your poo poo do all alone in this potty? "

Gracie shrugged, "I don't know." Then she regained strength and I felt the power shift back in her favor. "I don't want it to go yet."

Okay, Potty Training Mother, I thought, *do something.* Then I had an idea. We would give the poo poo a proper send-off by singing a song and doing the Poo Poo Happy Dance. A little party for the poo poo, so to speak. Perhaps then Gracie could let it go.

"A dance?" she asked when I explained my idea. "In the bathroom?"

"Why not?" I said. "I think your poo poo would love to see us do a Poo Poo Happy Dance and then send him on his way. What do you say?"

Long silence.

Even more silence. Then finally she said, "Okay."

Together, we sang about a happy poo poo, a pretty poo poo, Gracie's special poo poo, and did a conga-line dance around the bathroom chanting, "Flush the poo poo in the potty" over and over again. When the song was finished, Gracie pressed the little valve that let out a simulated flushing noise and a voice said, "Way to go." Gracie smiled. I respectfully lifted the little bucket out of the potty chair and delicately deposited the poo poo into the toilet. We offered a final salute and then Gracie did the honors by flushing the toilet.

The Poo Poo Happy Dance was repeated every time Gracie went to the bathroom for many weeks. It didn't matter which bathroom we were in—our own private one or a public restroom—Potty Training Mother faithfully sang and performed the Poo Poo Happy Dance. No doubt, many restaurant diners who happened to be seated close to the restrooms got to hear me saluting my daughter's poo poo. I didn't care because I was so thrilled to no longer be known as the Poo Poo Monster.

I'm sure my own mother would be proud to know that the money she spent on my singing and dancing lessons finally paid off.

Jumping on the Potty Train

By Kae

The myriad of *All the Goofy Advice About Babydom* books in my reference collection said that a well-adjusted child should be potty trained by the age of two. We were expecting our second child, so potty training Matthew became that much more important. The last thing I wanted to do was have two kids in diapers at the same time.

In November Matthew moved to the two-year-old room at daycare. I immediately was bombarded with the horror stories of mothers in the midst of the potty training nightmare. I was amazed to see these polished, in command, professional women tortured over when and where little Johnny made his poops.

My neighbor had a child in training at the time. Every time we saw each other I was treated to an in-depth update on her child's toilet habits. Frankly, I found this obsession with your child's waste to be somewhat disconcerting. My god, didn't these people have anything better to do with their time than sit around waiting for little Johnny to take a poop? Not to mention broadcasting this to everyone who would stand still to listen.

I was given literature from the daycare center that offered support groups and instructions on how to potty train. The mothers of the older two-year-olds in the room each had helpful hints to get me started on the road to a potty trained child: have the child go cold turkey and buy lots of laundry soap; use the potty seat on the floor first, then graduate up to the "big" potty; set a potty seat on top of the big potty; reward the child for going in the toilet and show disappointment for going any place else; don't let the child flush the toilet because the sound of the rushing water could scare him. It was quite overwhelming.

To top it all off, there appeared to be some type of competition among the daycare moms to see whose child would potty train first and fastest—as if taking a poop was an IQ indicator that determined the future bright and successful kids among the group.

I started Matthew on the "potty train," as he called it, in January. We lived in a suburb of Chicago, so David took the train to work every day. Sometimes on a Saturday David would take Matthew on the train and they would go into the city together. Matthew loved to ride on the train. When Matthew heard that we were going to start potty training, he assumed the two were related, and he was excited.

Since it was winter, we were indoors most of the time—eliminating the dreaded tantrums I had heard other mothers talk about when they had to drag their child away from the sandbox to use the bathroom.

For several weeks before beginning our trip on the "potty train," I let Matthew put various items in the toilet and watch them get flushed away. We started with mommy's deposits, big and little. Matthew pulled the handle and watched them swirl away. Then we put in toilet paper, breakfast cereal, and even marshmallows.

Once Matthew didn't want to eat his green beans, so down the big people potty they went. The simple act of watching the toilet paper swirl down the pipe made Matthew clap his hands and dance with glee.

I let Matthew sit on the closed lid of the toilet while I put on my makeup in the mornings, letting him get used to the feel. I let him sit on the toilet with the lid up just so he would know that he wouldn't fall in. To my amazement, he was not afraid of falling in or of the rushing water when the toilet was flushed. We talked every day about how fun it was going to be when Matthew got to wear big boy underpants and use the big boy toilet. He would clap his hands and proclaim, "I going to the potty train." I thought his reaction meant he was going to love using the big people potty. Wrong!

On Matthew's first day on the potty train, we went to the store and purchased some big boy underpants. We looked at all the little tidy whities with cartoon pictures on them. There was Batman, Spider-Man, and Scooby-Doo. Matthew chose Scooby. For many years to come, underpants in Matthew's world were called Scoobys.

"Matthew, today we are going to start potty training," I said as Matthew donned his new Scooby-Doo underpants. "If you have to go potty, we are using the big boy potty, okay?" I said this in my June Cleaver sweet voice (the one I had to work to develop). According to the *All the Goofy Advice About Babydom* books in my reference collection, everything evil in the world has been linked to negative feedback during the potty training stage. I was determined to make sure I did not earn any strikes in the potty training department.

"I going to the potty train," Matthew said as he danced around in his new Scooby underpants, clapping his little hands. I started the potty training exercise by putting Matthew on a strict potty schedule. Every 30 minutes I took him into the bathroom to see if nature was ready to call. The first time, nature eluded us and we left the bathroom without getting to flush the toilet—no giggle, no happy dance. The second time, same result. Every half an hour until lunch time, same result.

Matthew was sitting at the kitchen table eating his PB&J when I heard the sound of dripping water. Without even having to check, I knew that Scooby-Doo had been christened. "Matthew, why didn't you tell me you had to go potty?" I asked, less than thrilled but trying not to show it. "I eating my samich," Matthew informed me so seriously that I had to turn around so he didn't see me laughing.

"Mommy, when me going to the potty train?" Matthew asked as we stripped off the sodden pair of Scoobys and replaced them with a clean, dry pair. "Daddy going too?"

"Oh, Matthew, no. We are not going on the train. You are going to learn to go potty on the big boy potty. It's called potty training," I explained using my foreign June Clever voice.

As the realization dawned on Matthew that he had been lied to, that there was not going to be a fun ride on the train with his daddy, wearing his new Scooby-Doo underpants, he began to wail. "I go to potty train!" Matthew shrieked, threw himself on the floor, and had a whopper of a tantrum. Strike one.

Days turned into weeks. We had very few toilet flushes and happy dances. We had lots of pooping and peeing on Scooby. Matthew began to think of going to the bathroom as a burden and was resisting me at every turn. We would no sooner walk out of the bathroom than he would pee or poop on Scooby. I was quickly losing my June Cleaver mommy voice. Matthew's future therapy bill was looming large in my mind.

One day I realized that I was one of the walking wounded at the daycare center. I was in the middle of a group of mothers trading potty training horror stories and looking for solace. My child was not even on the radar for a daycare future that was bright and successful. Concerned that I was doing irreparable harm to both Matthew's psyche and my own, I called my dad. My dad was the chairman of the psychology department at Middle Tennessee State University. If anyone knew whether I was turning my child into a potential serial killer, it would be him.

My dad had the best advice I had ever heard for potty training. In his calm and quiet manner he asked me, "Do you know any 21-year-old people who are still wearing diapers?" It was all so clear. We all eventually learn to go to the bathroom and wipe our own butts. Matthew was obviously not responding to the "normal" methods of potty training. Surely I could find a way to get through to him that would be fun and less stressful for everyone concerned.

David and I developed reward systems to entice Matthew to make his "boom-boom" in the big boy toilet. In our house there were no cookies or candy, by ordinance of daddy. It was a rare and special occasion if Matthew was given candy. So we decided that each time he went to the potty on the big boy toilet, he would get a piece of candy. I purchased some Skittles and put them in a bowl behind each of our toilets. This technique worked very well. Matthew liked candy, and since he did not have any other way to get it, he was willing to attempt to do his business where he would be paid in fruity little tidbits.

All good things have a down side, though. Matthew liked getting his candy so much that he would sit and sit and sit on the toilet trying to go potty so that he would be rewarded. Of course, he couldn't be left in the bathroom alone, since technically he could fall into the toilet or fall off and hit his head, or otherwise hurt himself who knows how. Also, don't forget there was an entire bowl full of Skittles lurking right behind his head. So there we sat, waiting for nature to call. This was about as much fun and as quick as watching grass grow. So we made up a game. It was the "tell me questions" game—sort of like Jeopardy for a two-year-old.

David or I would quiz Matthew on all things a two-year-old might possibly know, and sometimes throw in some goofy things that he only thought he knew. Eventually Matthew would complete his potty trip, giggle and dance while watching the big flush, get his candy, and go skipping off.

Scooby-Doo was getting a break from the poop, but the pee was another story. Getting Matthew to pee in the toilet was impossible. He didn't understand that he was supposed to stand there and pee.

"Matthew, little boys stand up and go potty and girls sit down," I explained as I sat on the bathroom floor thinking of the ten thousand other things that I needed to do. "It's like dogs: Girl dogs squat and boy dogs lift their legs."

"I not go pee pee like this," Matthew said to me, putting one hand on my shoulder while hiking his leg up in the air like the dog next door when he wet on our front bushes.

"No, no, you don't have to stand on one leg," I giggled, despite my trying to be serious. "Little boys stand up because they have fire hoses and little girls don't." Matthew was totally into fire trucks at this age. He had a fire truck that had a hose that pulled out. I thought he might relate to this better.

This brings up another subject: Potty training brought with it the conflict of what to call all our private parts and actions. The myriad of parenting books in those days encouraged the use of ana-tomically correct terminology for these parts. This sounds fine on paper, but I just couldn't bring myself to yell the word "penis" down the hallway from our family room to the bathroom. We had to find our way to a more comfortable alternative, and "fire hose" it was.

I had truly become one of those moms who was obsessed with the peeing and pooping stage of child rearing. Sitting in the stu-dent lounge at school, I was regaling a group of my friends with Matthew's repeated lack of concern for Scooby's health and well-being when one of the boys told me how his mother got him to pee in the toilet. That afternoon during Matthew's nap I dropped several drops of dish soap into the toilet. When Matthew got up from his nap, I proceeded to load him up on fruit juice so that he would really have to pee. Finally nature called and we were about to do a magic trick.

"Just try it one time and see what happens," I said to Matthew as I pulled down his pants. Sure enough, he really had to go. He let his fire hose run full blast into the toilet. The force of the urine cre-ated yellow bubbles in the toilet. Matthew got so excited that he began clapping and dancing around. "Rein that fire hose in," I said as he danced his little jig, spraying his magic yellow bubble juice all over the bathroom.

From that day on, when Matthew had to urinate he would announce, "I have to go yellow bubbles." Then he would take his fire hose to the big boy potty. If minutes spent in the bathroom were dimes, I would be a wealthy woman living in a condo next to the ocean. I have logged countless hours on the edge of the bathtub playing "tell me questions." It was a sad day when the Skittles bowl was removed from service. All in all, Matthew was completely potty trained before his 21st birthday and appears not to have any emo-tional neurosis from my inept first ride on the potty train.

When it came time to train my second child, I waited. I didn't care that all the other kids were trained by 18 months. I didn't care that supposedly late potty training leads to less-than-desirable economic conditions in adulthood. I had been on that train and it was a nightmare I was not willing to repeat. So I waited. The age of two came and went. We looked at the big girl underpants at the store. We flushed various objects—but not the car keys—down the toilet. Matthew encouraged Christina, telling her about the Skittles on the back of the toilet. The truth was, Matthew wanted to reinstate the poop and reward system now that he had it down pat.

Finally, several months before Christina's third birthday, she began to show real interest in potty training. Off to the store we went to pick out big girl underpants. She picked out the pretty colored ones with lace frills on the bottoms.

Matthew tried to show her how to make yellow bubbles, but girls don't really get enough pressure going to make a good show of it. "It's okay, Steenie, I don't think girls can make yellow bubbles 'cause they don't have a fire hose," Matthew told Christina in his most serious big brother voice.

"What I got?" Christina wanted to know, looking down to where it was apparent she did not have a fire hose. I anxiously watched this exchange. Matthew had great imagination and I was sure this would be a whopper. "It's like your belly button, Steenie. Some got innies and some got outies. I got the outie."

"I pee pee from my belly button?" Christina said, now pulling her belly button out so she could see it more closely.

By now I'd collapsed onto the bathroom floor laughing and both kids turned to stare at me—Matthew with his fire hose out and Christina pulling on her belly button as if she had just discovered it.

"You're a girl, Steenie, girls can't make yellow bubbles standing up," Matthew said firmly.

"Can too."

"Can not."

"Can too."

"Can not."

"Can too, watch." Christina stood there and peed all over the bathroom floor. The warm puddle of yellow bubbles surrounded her little feet and Matthew did the Mexican Hat Dance into the bathtub to get out of the ever-spreading flow's way.

I grabbed the toilet paper and begin to sop up the yellow bubbles. "Christina Marie, don't you ever do that again, young lady. This is totally gross. Pee goes in the potty, not on the floor, not in your pants, and especially not in the bathtub." Both Matthew and Christina were wide-eyed when I begin my rant, but by the end they dissolved into giggles about peeing in the bathtub. *Great,* I thought, *give them another stunt to pull.* I put the saturated paper into the toilet. Christina, my little butterfly brain, said, "Oh good, it's time to flush!" She reached out and pulled the magic handle and the kids dissolved again into gales of giggles.

Matthew continued to help by playing the "tell me questions" game with Christina, and by her third birthday, her pretty little underpants with the lace frills on the bottom were safe—the majority of the time anyway.

Jack vs. the Toilet

By Pam

When it came time to potty train Jack, something wonderful and magical happened...he trained himself. I'd heard that the younger sibling often quickly learns from watching the older child, but I had fully expected that in our home, things would never come easily. I was pleasantly surprised. Just before Jack turned two years old, he walked over to Gracie's potty chair, dropped his drawers, sat down, and whizzed. He even had the presence of mind to direct his penis in the right direction. He then stood up triumphantly and ran over to me for a congratulatory hug. In his excitement, though, he neglected to pull his underwear and pants back up, so he fell head first onto the bathroom rug after the first step.

His bump on the head didn't deter him, however, and he became a quick study. From that first moment of whizzing success, he peed in the potty every time. Gracie was still wearing pull-ups at night and Jack was wearing underpants 24/7 because he never had an accident. Once he knew that the potty was where the pee pee belonged, he was eager to pee with the best of them. He even quickly mastered the step stool in front of the big toilet and was sitting there on his throne, proud as could be. I was thrilled.

I also knew I should enjoy this now, because there would come a time in the near future when I'd have to let Jack in on a little secret: He could pee standing up. I was hoping to hold off as long as possible because I valued the cleanliness of my bathroom, but he'd eventually find out. For now, though, I was very happy that I didn't have to sit on the edge of the tub for an hour, trying to convince my child to surrender one drop of pee into the potty.

After a few days of peeing proudly in the toilet, Jack was ready for the next step. He announced that he had to poo poo. My memories of Gracie being terrified of having her poo poo flushed down the toilet were still fresh in my mind, so I was ready to be as delicate and sensitive as possible. I didn't know what poo poo issues Jack might have, but I was going to be ready for them. I would not be insensitive to his poo poo. I never wanted to be referred to as the Poo Poo Monster again.

Jack, however, didn't care what his poo poo's destiny was after he was through with it. I don't know whether it was a boy thing or just a Jack thing, but he was very matter-of-fact about it. He pooped, he wiped, he flushed, he washed, end of story...almost.

To this day I don't understand how a small child—a picky eater at that—could produce the mega poo he did. But as he was washing his hands, I heard the sound of a toilet in trouble. Our dependable toilet, which had successfully swallowed up many things not meant to ever be flushed down a toilet, was losing the battle when it came to Jack's poo.

I leaned back from the sink and nervously peered into the toilet. The tide was rising up, up, up, dangerously close to the rim of the bowl. Obviously, Jack's poo poo was not going down without a fight.

"Mommy, what's wrong?" Jack asked as he looked at the reflection of my worried face in the bathroom mirror.

"Nothing, honey," I responded lightly. I didn't want his first poo poo experience to be a bad one, with him feeling he had caused a flood or broke the toilet.

The rising water in the toilet had stopped, so I knew we weren't in danger of a flood. I ushered Jack out of the bathroom, gave him a treat for his first successful poo poo in the potty, and set him up with some toys. Then I headed back to the bathroom, closed and locked the door behind me, and prepared to tackle the toilet.

After working the plunger for several moments, the dam finally burst and the toilet flushed freely. I washed my hands, left the bathroom, and completely forgot about the incident by the end of the day. Perhaps it had just been a one-time quirky thing. Toilets do malfunction every now and then.

Then came day two. Jack announced he had to poo poo and we both happily went into the bathroom so he could do what all big boys do. Sitting on the toilet, he grunted, groaned, turned red in the face, and then smiled victoriously when he had finished. He wiped, he flushed, he washed, and again, the toilet made that familiar gurgling sound as it announced it was not going to send Jack's poo poo speeding down the pipes and into the septic tank. I looked at the familiar sight of the rising water and breathed a sigh of relief when it stopped short of overflowing.

I looked at my small son and looked back at the toilet. How could this be? How could this little child have such an effect on a toilet that had served our family well for so many years?

Day three: When Jack announced that he had to poo poo, I stood next to him so I could see the evidence for myself before he attempted to flush. I stared at his poo poo. It looked normal, it just looked big...*very, very big*.

"Why are you looking at my poo poo, Mommy?" Jack asked.

"Uh, no reason, really," I said as I realized we were now both standing over the toilet, gazing into the water.

"Is my poo poo bad?" he asked in a worried tone.

"It's a fine poo poo, Jack, " I answered as I prepared to flush. "It's a very fine poo poo, indeed."

Flush, gurgle, gurgle.

For the third straight day, the plunger was put into use.

I called the doctor later that day and he said that if Jack didn't appear constipated or uncomfortable, he was probably fine. Add more fiber to his diet, the doctor recommended. We also made an appointment for a check-up, just to be sure there wasn't anything wrong.

After Jack's check-up revealed he was in perfect health with a squeaky clean digestive system, we were sent home with instructions to make sure he drank enough water and ate a good amount of vegetables. Trying to get vegetables into him was already a source of stress, so the idea of having to get *more* vegetables into him was, at that point, beyond my ability to comprehend. I knew, though, that we couldn't carry a plunger with us wherever we went, and I certainly didn't want Jack to have difficulty taking care of business. So I devised a plan. I would use the only trick I could think of that might get him to open his steel-trap jaws and swallow vegetables: I would *disguise* them!

On the drive home from the doctor's office, I made a detour to the book store. I headed straight for the cookbook section and methodically searched and searched until I found what I was after. I knew there had to be the kind of cookbook I was looking for because I certainly couldn't be the only mother who was clueless about how to get vegetables into her children without a battle. And there was a cookbook exactly like that on the shelf (in fact, there was more than one)—a cookbook designed solely for deception. A cookbook filled with disguised vegetable recipes. I hugged the book to my chest and joyfully walked to the cashier.

At home, I read through the book, made a shopping list, and then headed to the supermarket to stock up on ingredients.

During the next week I sliced, diced, shredded, and pureed a variety of vegetables. They were carefully embedded in burgers, layered into casseroles, and covered with cheese. The food processor that hadn't been used since my baby food–making attempt years ago was working overtime. Every day you could hear all these happy little Martha Stewart sounds coming from my kitchen as I created a vast assortment of healthy, vegetable-filled meals.

Just as the cookbook author promised, my kids willingly ate the food and were none the wiser. I was happy and felt like such a good mother because I was ensuring that my children were getting adequate amounts of healthy, fresh vegetables.

Even though I was thrilled with what was going into Jack's body, I was less than impressed with what was coming out the other end. Jack's poo poos were still causing plumbing distress.

Whenever we had plans to visit someone, I would time the visit for after Jack had pooped. Although I was getting used to having a stopped-up toilet, I didn't think it was fair to have my child cause plumbing issues for friends and relatives.

During outings to restaurants, when Jack declared he had to go poo poo, I would nervously walk him to the restroom and keep my fingers crossed the whole time he pooped. He never caused a blockage problem at a restaurant restroom, but I'm assuming that's because they have industrial-strength plumbing. That wasn't the case at preschool, though.

One afternoon when I went to pick Jack up from preschool, he wasn't in his classroom. I looked around and was told by one of the aides that he was in the bathroom doing "number two." Uh-oh! Normally Jack was a late afternoon pooper, so we were always home by then. This time, however, he had to go earlier than usual. I walked into the bathroom to see Jack and his teacher staring at the rising water in the toilet. Instinctively, I looked around for a plunger.

"Oh goodness, we have a problem," Jack's teacher said in a concerned voice.

"Oh don't worry," said Jack, "this happens all the time. Mommy can fix it."

The teacher looked at me and I gave her a weak smile.

Apparently, toilet mishaps are a normal occurrence in preschool, so the teachers are well-equipped to handle it. Jack's teacher immediately went into action and a flood was averted.

Over the next few months, Jack continued to faithfully use the toilet without any accidents and I continued to plunge. We even had some days where my overworked plunger couldn't handle the job and Scott had to use the heavy-duty toilet snake. Of course, when Scott told the kids that he was putting a snake in the toilet, they screamed. When you're potty training children, the last thing you need is your helpful husband announcing that a snake is going in the same place where they will be sitting bare-bottomed.

One day, for no apparent reason I can think of, Jack's poo poos started becoming more cooperative. I can only assume his digestive system matured. Who knows? Things just started becoming normal again, and the plunger and snake were only brought into use on rare occasions. However, I often still say silent prayers for peaceful plumbing whenever a toilet is flushed.

Preschool or Bust

By Kae

By the time Jessica, my third child, approached the age for potty training, I was a jaded mother of almost nine years. I had taken the trip on the potty train twice and was in no hurry whatsoever to get on again. As long as Jessica was potty trained before she left for college, everything would be good by me.

Jessica is my strong-minded child. In some circles she would possibly be considered stubborn. With this character trait in mind, I knew that until she was ready, there was no sense in wasting my energy and emotions trying to get her to do something she didn't want to do. This was Jessica we were talking about. She was as stubborn as a mule. If it wasn't her idea, it wasn't going to happen without a fight. So we waited.

Of course, I made the requisite attempts to interest her in potty training. We talked about her being the only person in the house who wore diapers. We went to the store and looked at the pretty underpants. I even resorted to making sure she knew that only babies wore diapers. From the time Jessica learned to talk, her mantra was, "I'm not a baby," so I thought that would be a convincing argument. She didn't care a bit. That is, until Christina went to first grade.

The morning Christina started first grade, I came downstairs to find Jessica sitting at the kitchen table eating a bowl of cereal. She was completely dressed in one of her cutest outfits and had a backpack and a lunch box packed with food on the table next to her.

"Well, look who's up and moving early this morning," I said as I assessed the situation. "Why are you up so early, little miss britches?"

"I'm getting ready for school."

"You don't go to school." I grabbed a cup from the cupboard and filled it to the rim with coffee. I had the distinct feeling I was going to need it.

"Yes I do. Today I get to go to school with Matthew and Christina."

"Jessica, you're only three. You have to be five to go to school with Matthew and Christina." This statement was met with Jessica's big dark eyes. The storm was brewing.

"No! Christina was in kindergarten and now she is in first grade. That means I get to go to kindergarten today." Jessica folded her arms across her chest. The mule had entered the room.

"Jessica, it's the law. You have to be five to go to kindergarten."

"That's not fair. I'm not a baby. I'm ready to go to school like Matthew and Christina."

Jessica and I spent the majority of the rest of the day arguing about her going to school. Finally, I calmed her down by saying we would see if she could go to preschool a couple of days a week with other kids her own age. I found out that there was a great Montessori school about a block away, literally around the corner from our house. I called and made an appointment to tour the facilities on Friday afternoon. Jessica was thrilled.

After Jessica's nap on Friday, David, she and I walked over to meet the director of the preschool. We had a wonderful tour of the facilities. Jessica was very excited and couldn't stop pulling on my hand and pointing to all the exciting activities the other children were engaged in. We asked if they had a spot for her and the director looked right at Jessica and said, "We have a spot for a three-year-old, but you are not potty trained. We don't take children in diapers."

Jessica didn't miss a beat. She put her hands on her hips and looked directly up into the director's eyes. "If I don't pee my pants 'til Monday, can I come?"

The director was clearly taken aback with the directness of the question, but said, "Yes, yes you can. But you can't wear a diaper anymore."

"See you Monday," Jessica said as she began marching toward home, David and me racing behind her to catch up before she had to cross the street. Jessica walked straight to our house, marched into Christina's bedroom, opened her underwear drawer, and pulled out a pair of underpants. She pulled off her pants, ripped off the diaper, put on Christina's underpants, and pulled her pants back on. "Okay, now I am a big girl wearing big girl pants. I can go to school on Monday."

Believe it or not, that was it. Jessica donned her sister's underpants and she never had a single accident, day or night. We must have gotten on the express potty train this time.

Chapter 5

Public Humiliation

Public Restrooms

By Pam

O nce your toddler gets over the fascination of what should and shouldn't be flushed down the toilet, and the fact that he or she can climb onto the step stool by the sink and turn the faucet on and off and on and off or squeeze every last drop out of the toothpaste tube, your home bathroom becomes just another room in the house. Public restrooms, however, hold a never-ending fascination for the toddler mind. Public restrooms have a variety of flushing configurations, varying sink heights, adventurous hand-drying options, hypnotic echoes, and *other people!*

Public restrooms also provide mothers with yet more opportunities to fear for our children's health and become hopelessly embarrassed by what our children say and do. It's also during the countless trips we make accompanying our little ones to the restroom that we resign ourselves to the fact that it will be years before we will once again be able to enjoy a hot restaurant meal.

My children had particular favorites when it came to public restrooms. They knew exactly which ones had automatic flushing and automatic hand dryers. For Jack, the fact that the toilet "knew" to flush whenever he stepped away from it sent him into a fit of giggles. The "magic eye" of the toilet was something he was determined to outsmart. For my daughter, telling her that the toilet had a magic eye created hysterical crying and fear that the toilet was watching her poo poo. My mistake. I explained to her that it wasn't really an eye, but rather, a sensor. That frightened her just as much because she was sure a monster was putting laser beams in her back while she sat on the toilet. So mommy had to put her finger over the sensor the entire time we were in the stall.

The first time Jack realized that other people could use the restroom at the same time as him became an opportunity for social interaction. "What 'cha doin' in there?" Jack whispered to the stall divider. There was no response. "I see your feet, I know you're there," he continued.

"Jack, ssssh. Everyone deserves their own privacy. Now do your business and let's get going," I said. Just then, there was an unmistakable plopping sound in the toilet next door. I looked at Jack, put my hand over his mouth, and shook my head. It did no good. I knew Jack's comment was inevitable. Poop commentary is too irresistible for a young boy.

"Ooh, mommy, that person made a big stinky," he announced as he pried my hand away.

"Jack, ssssh," I repeated. Then I waited until I was sure that person had exited the restroom before we came out of the stall.

The independent streak in Gracie was fueled by public restrooms. Even though she lived in mortal fear of the toilet's magic eye, she loved the sensors on the faucets and hand dryers because it allowed her to act like a grown-up in front of other people. The same sensor that terrified her on the toilet amused her at the automatic paper towel dispenser. Apparently, when you have your pants around your ankles the sensor is more sinister, but when you're fully clothed, you've leveled the playing field. She was convinced that just jumping up and waving hello to the dispenser caused it to send a towel down her way. The future little bathroom attendant loved offering to get towels for anyone approaching to wash their hands.

During potty training, an outing to restaurants was a game of mommy-jump-up whenever my kids even hinted that they might have to pee or poo. There were many outings when my husband spent much of the time alone at a table set for four, eating his dinner by himself as I spent much of the evening in the restroom. It got to the point where we would always invite Scott's parents out to dinner with us just so he'd have someone to talk to while I was gone.

When dining out, we also learned to ask for the table nearest the restroom. We'd forego sitting at the lovely table with the view just to cut down on how much walking I'd have to do through the restaurant with two wiggly children. As far as I was concerned, I defined optimum table location by whether I could clearly see the restroom signs.

I was well aware of which restrooms my children loved and which ones were just plain old bathrooms. Whenever we ventured out to a restaurant or store, I knew in advance whether we'd be making the normal single visit or if this would be a multi-visit venture, based on bathroom interest. At the restaurants with the best bathrooms, I simply ordered a salad and gave up any dreams of a hot meal.

Now, you may be thinking to yourself that I should've put my foot down and announced that there would be one trip and one trip only to the restroom. That may have worked for other mothers, but the gastrointestinal tracts of the Bennett children defied logic. One night at our favorite restaurant Jack announced that he had to go poo poo. I sternly looked over at him and said that he had already been to the restroom twice and he'd have to wait until dinner was over. Moments later, an unmistakable odor filled the air and an unmistakable substance filled his underwear. Being stern wasn't worth the clean-up I had to do.

Public restrooms also created quite a challenge for the germophobe in me. Taking two children into the stall at the same time and attempting to help one out of their pants and safely onto the potty, while making sure the other one touched nothing, was quite a circus act.

"Don't touch *anything*!" I announced to the children as we entered the restroom. Once inside the stall, I pulled out a disposable potty cover to lay over the toilet seat. If you ever wonder why I carry such a large purse, it's because I have an entire package of potty covers as well as hand sanitizer, disinfecting wipes, and travel-size Lysol spray in my purse. Does that qualify me as an official germophobe? I think so.

Once I got the potty cover situated, I carefully placed one of the children on the toilet. If that child was Gracie, I also put my finger over the toilet sensor. All the while, I had to keep an eye on Jack so he wouldn't touch anything. With Jack, I also had to make sure he wasn't peering under the stall to wave to the person next door. Until my children were old enough to go into two separate bathroom stalls, I also had to constantly remind one child to stay turned away from the sibling on the potty to ensure privacy.

For my children, public restrooms held another fascinating feature. They seemed to be the one place where they loved to reminisce. It's while on the toilet in the public restroom that my children would remind me (loudly) about the time daddy farted at the family picnic or mommy's shirt button popped open and everyone could see my bra.

It was also in the public restroom that Gracie showed her sweet, understanding side. When she was starting potty training, she would become alarmed at the odor coming from her poo. I repeatedly had to reassure her that everybody's poo poo stinks. That became a saying she would use whenever she pooped. As we flushed the toilet, she'd look at me and say, "Mommy, everybody's poo poo stinks, right?"

"Right," I agreed.

Gracie apparently was concerned that others in the public restroom might be concerned about odor as well, so whenever someone emerged from the stall, she'd gently reassure them by saying, "It's okay m'am, everybody's poo poo stinks."

Animal Crackers

By Kae

Running errands takes on a new meaning when you become a mother. In fact, it should no longer be called "running" errands. When you have a child, getting out of the house and into the car can be quite an ordeal. Once you get to your destination, the ordeal resumes in reverse. Going anywhere with a two-year-old is like having a surprise party at every turn.

On top of that, children are, by nature, the very definition of bipolar. They can swing from giggling and happy to crying and traumatized in a nanosecond. As adults we are woefully ill-equipped to follow the ups and downs of our toddlers' mood swings.

I was careful to plan the timing of our outings. The best times to run errands were first thing in the morning and early in the afternoon. First thing in the morning, the children have eaten and generally made their "boom-boom" for the morning. They are fully rested and nap time is several hours away. The same holds true for afternoon errand runs. They have just gotten up from their naps and have had a snack before leaving the house. Generally, the daily "boom-boom" has already occurred after breakfast, but if not, surely after lunch.

Why, you ask, is it important to know the "boom-boom" schedule? Because at the age of two, I was deep in the throes of attempting to potty train my son, because all the books on Super Momdom-Super Childdom said that well-adjusted children should be potty trained by the age of two. My mother-in-law had potty trained her children by 18 months. It seemed to me that when Matthew turned two, women came out of the woodwork to enlighten me about how I was late for the potty train. So I became obsessed that Matthew would be developmentally slow because I had not pursued his potty training with the proper diligence.

Please remember that this was during the 1980s. We didn't have such things as pull-ups. We went straight from diapers to Scooby-Doo underwear. The last thing you want to do is be in the line at the dry cleaner and be greeted with the wafting aroma that undeniably announces your child has pooped on Scooby. Not only is this uncomfortable for child and adults standing in the line, but it creates a logistical nightmare getting said child back into his car seat for the trip home.

One other major problem that can occur on an ill-timed outing is the dreaded tantrum. I had heard about tantrums from other parents. I had actually witnessed several tantrums—by other people's children—in the grocery store or in my neighbor's front yard as we stood on the sidewalk talking. One thing I noticed about tantrums was that they seemed to happen when the child felt they were not being attended to properly or, the more common cause, the child was not getting what they wanted at the exact moment they wanted it.

I was always amazed at how parents made excuses for their child's behavior instead of correcting it. A child would be having a fit, rolling around on the ground and screaming like a banshee. The parent would turn to the child, pull the kid in to their side, and say, "Oh, you're just tired." I actually heard a parent at the daycare center say to her child, "You can have this candy, but you are just going to be wild from the sugar." Sure enough, the instant the child finished the candy, the bad behavior began. I raised my children to understand that they were expected to behave properly, period. It didn't matter if they were tired or had just eaten candy or drank a Coke. There was no excuse for bad behavior.

I set a few things in motion to cut down on the number of tantrums I would have to endure. The first thing I did was decide that if this was an attention ploy, then I would not give attention to the child, positive or negative. During the tantrum stage, I dressed my children in overalls. When a tantrum was in the wind-up phase, I would pick the child up by the yolk in the back and carry them at arm's length to their crib and leave them there. I would only say, "When you're done, I'll be back." With that, I would close the bedroom door and continue with what I was doing until I heard no more "unacceptable" noises coming from the room. When I opened the door I always asked, "Are you done?" The child would nod their head yes and I would pick them up and spend a few minutes of undivided time with them. This usually involved a little game or just a cuddle session.

Even when you plan everything out carefully, though, the bipolar child can emerge when you least expect it. On this day, I had spent the morning at school, picked Matthew up from daycare, and entertained (briefly) the idea that since the grocery store was only a few blocks away from his daycare center, I could do a little shopping. I was tired from being in classes all morning and rushing to pick Matthew up before the half-day rate turned into the full-day rate at daycare. I was loaded down with homework and would have to stay up late that night to get it done. I also *had* to go to the grocery store.

I hate going to the grocery store more than anything else I have to do. I will wait until there is nothing in the refrigerator, pantry, or freezer, and only then grudgingly go to the store to restock. This was one of these times. I think we may have had ketchup in the fridge and that was it. There was no option to wait until a later date. Today was the day for groceries.

Knowing full well that taking a two-year-old directly from day-care to the grocery store was parental suicide, I drove home for play time, nap time, and snack time. When Matthew went down for his nap I got a head start on my homework, even though a nap was calling my name loudly from our upstairs bedroom. When Matthew woke up, we had our after-nap snuggle and then a snack.

Matthew was going to be a big brother and I had no intention of having two children in diapers at the same time, so we were very deep in the throes of potty training. After the nap and snack, we spent an inordinate amount of time in the upstairs bathroom waiting for nature to take its course. If nature hasn't called, it's very important to wait if you want to go spend an hour in the grocery store incident-free. Finally, nature's call had been answered and Scooby was safe to make the trip.

Normally when we went to the store, Matthew would sit in the front seat of the cart holding the grocery list and be perfectly content to pretend he was reading the list and pointing at the various items he hoped I would drop into the cart. I would keep us both entertained by asking what color the fruit was and pretending I didn't know my apples from my grapes so Matthew could clear up the question for me. We would squeeze the bath tissue to see which one was softest. Matthew was always partial to Charmin. I think he just liked the color on the wrapper, but he swore it was the softest of all the tissues so it was the one that went into the cart.

This particular day would not be normal.

Matthew was holding the grocery list and pointing down the first several aisles. We were filling the cart at record speed. We had gotten to the cracker aisle and Matthew began to whine. He wanted to get the animal crackers, but the budget was slim this week and the answer had to be no. Every child has a precursor to the upcoming tantrum. Matthew had a distinctive, plaintive whine that would creep into his normally sweet little voice.

And so the nightmare began. First it was the "why, why, why" and then the legs started to kick. Once the legs were in motion, there was no holding back the tidal wave. Matthew opened his mouth and drew in a long breath, held it for a split second, then did his best imitation of an air raid siren right in the middle of the cracker aisle. His feet began banging against the metal grate of the grocery cart. For some reason, this reminded me of a wild animal attempting to regain its freedom from a metal cage.

"Matthew, if you don't stop it I am going to get angry," I said in my stern mother's voice I really didn't have to practice much to obtain.

"I going home, *now*," Matthew wailed in response, over and over again in a chanting cadence accented with the rhythmic clanging of the metal cart as he pounded it with his sneakers.

Everyone in the cracker aisle stopped what they were doing and glared in our direction. I did the only rational thing: I fled. I raced my cart to the front of the store to the customer service counter. The look on the girl's face was one of sheer terror as I brought this hysterical child wailing and banging up to the desk. I lifted Matthew from the cart, artfully dodging several blows with the flailing feet, and asked the wide-eyed clerk if she could watch my cart; I would be back.

The truth is, I had no intention of ever coming back to that store. I would start shopping in the next suburb over, I was so embarrassed. My first intention was to flee directly to my car, put Matthew in his car seat, and drive home as quickly as possible. I would call my husband at work and have him pick up Chinese food on his way home from the train and we could try the shopping thing again tomorrow in the next town.

Then I realized that if I let Matthew dictate at the age of two when we left the store, I would be doomed for life. His behavior was totally unacceptable and I was ever so close to rewarding this behavior by taking him home—which was just what he wanted.

I opened the car door and Matthew pulled one spectacular bipolar show and became all Mr. Giggles and Sunshine. We were going home! To his surprise, he was treated to a gentle but firm dose of psychology applied directly to his backside.

"You will not, under any circumstance, act this way in public. Do you understand me?" I said in my stern momma voice that was to become legend within our household.

Matthew nodded his head. I am pretty sure he had no idea what I had just said to him. What he did know was that the tone of my voice, the look on my face, and the pat on the poah-poah clearly indicated in two-year-oldese that all was not well.

I took Matthew's hand and led him back into the store. Once inside, I found our cart and put Matthew back in the front seat and handed him the grocery list. "I want you to say you're sorry to the lady for making her watch our cart when that is not her job."

"Sorry, lady," Matthew said and turned his charming red-rimmed blue eyes on her. The look on her face said all was forgiven.

"So, what aisle were we on?"

"Animal cracker aisle," Matthew said as I pushed the cart back to the place we had been before we were so rudely interrupted.

Discipline is one of the hardest aspects of parenting. Some parents take the path of least resistance, giving in to the child's every whim and fancy under the guise of keeping the peace. Other parents yell at their children over and over and over and then never follow up with anything concrete, so the kids just learn to tune them out.

On this day, I was sitting at the crossroads and I chose to be the adult in my relationship with my child. I chose not to be a peer or an equal. I chose to be a parent. Tantrums may be a normal part of being two/three years old, but that does not mean they should be accepted. Even if the behavior is "normal," it is still unacceptable, and as a parent I felt it was my job to communicate this to my child in a way that he would understand.

I'd like to say this was the only tantrum Matthew ever threw and that because I took control, I saved myself from this particular parental trauma. The truth is, Matthew and my other children all threw their fair share of tantrums. Tears were shed, wails reverberated off walls, and doses of gentle but firm psychology were administered liberally to the seats of pants. I will say that I think compared to some of my friends and acquaintances, my children had fewer tantrums. After a couple of episodes, a look with raised eyebrows was about enough to make them at least weigh the advantages and disadvantages of the impending tantrum. It was always fun to watch them decide it just wasn't worth it and move on.

A Fire Hose by Any Other Name

By Pam

Kae and I agree on many parenting issues and she, in fact, has been the voice of sanity (yes, believe it or not) during my most trying times. One area where we differ, though, is the naming of body parts. My approach is to call it what it is. Rather than have the words *penis* and *vagina* become mystical or giggly words for my kids, I figured we'd just start out with the correct names. I assumed I was being a mature, practical mother.

Kae took a different route with her kids. She chose such interesting descriptions as *fire hose*. I don't know how she ever explained what firefighters used to put out fires, but as far as I was concerned, I was taking the no-nonsense approach.

Looking back, perhaps Kae's fire hose approach was safer.

When we first brought Jack home, Gracie, who was two years old, was understandably interested in being mommy's little helper with her baby brother. She happily assisted in bathing and feeding him. Bath time was when Gracie first brought up the question of why Jack looked different than she did. Being the mature mother, I quite simply explained that Jack had a penis and Gracie had a vagina. She couldn't pronounce either word, but seemed perfectly happy with my brief explanation. During each bath we would work on pronouncing all our body parts, and Gracie was getting better at proper identification. The word vagina was still beyond her ability, and she was, in fact, stuck on referring to it as a "giant," but she could easily say penis whenever she felt the need.

When we brought Jack home at four and a half months old, he had not been circumcised. Apparently, circumcision isn't the norm in Guatemala. On the advice of our pediatrician, however, we chose to have Jack circumcised. It would be minor surgery and it was recommended that we wait until he was at least six or seven months old to reduce anesthesia risks. Our plan was to have Jack circumcised after the winter holidays. So Gracie's first peek at Jack in the buff was when he was still uncircumcised.

That year, we planned a large Christmas party for our friends and also my husband's employees and business associates. My mother helped by preparing several of her traditional holiday appetizers. Everyone was having a great time and my two kids were the center of attention. Many of Scott's business associates were meeting our children for the first time. I was the proud mother indeed!

I was sitting in the center of the living room with Gracie on my lap when my mother walked in and set down a tray of appetizers on the coffee table. The tray was filled with all kinds of hot, delicious food. For as long as I can remember, my mother always loved serving her pigs in a blanket, which consisted of mini frankfurters wrapped in flaky dough. Her pigs in a blanket were arranged neatly in the center of the tray. All conversation stopped momentarily as everyone eyed the delicious array of food. Gracie hopped off my lap, closely inspected the tray, and made an important announcement to the quiet room.

"Mommy, that looks like Jack's penis," she called out, pointing to the pigs in a blanket. "There are so many penises on that dish." It was then that I wished I had followed Kae's advice and called it a fire hose!

Some people who were just about to pop the mini frankfurters into their mouths abruptly stopped and tried to discreetly place them back down on their plates. Others eyed the tray suspiciously. No one wanted to be the first one to take a bite. The innocent pigs in a blanket had suddenly taken on a whole new persona.

I quickly slid off the couch and grabbed another tray from the kitchen counter. "Anyone interested in some cheese and crackers?" I asked.

Chapter 6

Because I Said So

The Discipline Wars

By Kae

First off, let me tell you that my husband and I are not just spouses but also best friends. We can talk for hours and still have things left to say to each other at the end of the day. What we are not is the same. We have different opinions on politics—one is a Democrat, the other a Republican. We have somewhat similar but also significantly different views about religion. We don't like the same music or movies. But on the basics of life, we are almost always on the same page and most often on the same sentence. We agree on the types of houses we like, the furniture we like, the vacations we like to go on, how to run our finances, where we want to be at different stages of our lives, and on and on and on.

The one thing we don't agree on and will never agree on is how to discipline our children. This colossal difference in parenting styles made itself apparent on Matthew's second Christmas.

Matthew was 14 months old and Christmas was just another day for him. For David, this was his first Christmas with a child and he was up with the birds and wired for sound. David woke Matthew up singing off-key Christmas carols. Then it was time to see what Santa Claus had left under the tree. Matthew opened his first gift, a pint-size Notre Dame football. Matthew played as much with the brightly colored wrapping paper and curly ribbon as he did his new toys, but he was happy and so were we. It was a wonderful first Christmas together. After opening presents, David and Matthew played with the toys while I made breakfast. We ate and played and eventually it was time to get ready to go to David's parents' house for the family Christmas meal.

"Matthew, we have to get a bath and get ready to go to grandma's house," I said to him, as if at 14 months old he was going to be able to understand what I was saying. I reached down and picked him up from the pile of glittery wrapping paper and ribbons. This is where the trouble began. Matthew began kicking his feet and started to cry. For a lot of parents this reaction would be normal. For me, it was surprising. Matthew was a very content child, once we got the lactose intolerance and scratchy clothes issues resolved. He would sit in the same place for hours, perfectly happy to play with one toy. This reaction was very unusual.

Not giving in to his crying, I took him into the bathroom and shut the door. I didn't shut the door to keep David from being disturbed while he cleaned up our wrapping mess and breakfast dishes; I shut the door to corral the child who was scrambling to get back to his presents.

Once safely in the bathroom, I tried to distract Matthew with one of his favorite activities, brushing his teeth. I would make a big show of Matthew helping me get his toothbrush, always making sure to pick up mine or David's first so that Matthew could shake his head no and point to his toothbrush in the cup. Then I would carefully put the toothpaste on and ask Matthew, "Is that right?" He would nod his head yes and open his mouth like a chick getting food from its mother. I would put the toothbrush in his mouth. He would grasp it in his tiny little hand, trying to do his best to act like he was brushing, usually resulting in toothpaste up his nose, which always made him giggle. But not today.

Today Matthew was having none of it. He would not help pick out his toothbrush, and when I tried to put it in his mouth he let it fall to the floor. "Well, Matthew," I said, somewhat bemused by this behavior. I ran the water for the tub. I picked Matthew up by the shoulders and set him firmly on the closed lid of the toilet. Putting my index finger on one cheek and my thumb on the other, I applied just enough pressure to pop his mouth open. Then I inserted the toothbrush I had retrieved from the floor—and, in my defense, actually rinsed off and re-applied fresh toothpaste—into his mouth and finished the job of brushing his little pearly whites.

With Matthew at this age, any firm display of displeasure from me was enough to calm him down and get him to start acting "normal" again. But not today.

Today, getting Matthew out of his pajamas and into the buff was like wrestling a monkey slathered in Wesson oil. The pajamas of choice in this cold and snowy climate had a high collar like a mock turtleneck, with three snaps on the side to provide enough space for the kid's head to poke through. The wrists were like tennis wristbands made of elastic to keep the sleeves down over the tender little arms of babies not old enough to be able to yank their own sleeves down when they got cold. The pajama bottoms ended in cute little plastic feet that had fuzzy material in them to keep the little one's tootsies toasty during the night. There were snaps along the waistband of the pants that held the top and the bottom together.

On a normal day it took a parent with a degree in quantum physics to figure out how to get Matthew in and out of those pajamas. Today, I needed to call in the SWAT team to subdue the squirmy little fellow. And to top off the whole experience, the last obstacle between me and Matthew in his birthday suit was a diaper that had missed a scheduled changing. When the pajama bottoms came off, it was quickly apparent that not all the packages had been left under the tree.

After a constant dialogue of "Matthew cut it out," "What is wrong with you?" "That's enough," and maybe a couple of expletives—okay several expletives that have been deleted here—Matthew was stripped, brushed, wiped and ready for a bath.

On a normal day, Matthew sat in the tub and played with his toys while I washed his various parts. Then he'd get to take a turn with the washcloth, washing all his parts again. I would ask, "Did you wash under your arms?" and he would rub the cloth under each of his armpits. "Did you wash behind your ears?" and he would wash behind each of his ears. "Did you get the lint out of your belly button?" At this, Matthew would pull out his belly button, look intently, and always give me a big grin. I would wash his hair, being ever so careful not to get any water on his face. Matthew hated water on his face. We had a bathroom that was so small that if you turned around, you bumped into yourself. Trust me, the last thing you needed in there was a high-pitched scream that could break glass. (Rock concerts are not the leading cause of hearing loss in women; it's shrieking children in small bathrooms.) On most days, bath time at the Allen house was great fun. But not today.

Today, I put Matthew in the tub and immediately he began flailing his feet and arms, sending great plumes of water out of the tub all over the floor. One unintended consequence of this flailing was copious amounts of water hitting Matthew directly in the face. The air raid siren went off. I snatched a towel from the rod and wiped his face as quickly as possible, but the sound had already penetrated my brain. "Well, that's what you get for flailing around like a crazy person," I said to Matthew as I systematically scrubbed all his parts. I gave him the washcloth but he just threw it on the floor pretty much where the toothbrush had landed.

Matthew began to calm down a little bit, until he saw me reach over for the shampoo bottle. "No, no, no, no, no" he started, and the siren was sounding again. So I washed his hair fast and furious. I snatched him out of the tub all clean and shiny, wrapped him in a towel, and handed him to David to dress.

Believe it or not, I had maintained my cool up to this point. I understood that he was excited because it was Christmas and he didn't want to leave all his new toys to take a bath. I thought the faster I could get finished with what had to be done, the quicker he could be back in the living room playing with his toys.

Sure enough, when I finished getting myself cleaned up in the bathroom, David and Matthew were both playing happily and all was well in the Allen house once again. Until we had to leave.

Did I mention this was Chicago in December? There was snow on the ground and the temperature was frigid. Matthew would have to wear a snowsuit. It was way too cold to go outside in nothing but a coat. I was trying to wrestle Matthew into his snowsuit when he began shouting, "No, no, no, no" at the top of his lungs and trying to wrench free from me.

And that was it. That was all I was going to take from this pint-size monster. I grabbed him firmly by the arm, turned him around, and applied a light smack to the bottom of his pants. "That is enough," I said in a stern voice, emphasizing each word. Matthew had never been in any real trouble before, and he was momentarily caught off guard by this swat on the bottom. He stopped screaming and thrashing. Until David came around the corner from the kitchen wearing what I lovingly refer to as his "dark face" and boomed, "Don't you spank him! It's Christmas!"

"I don't care if it's his birthday, he can't act like this," I said as I continued tugging the pants of the snowsuit up Matthew's legs.

"You are not going to spank our kids. If he doesn't want to wear a snowsuit, he doesn't have to," David said.

Just like that, our colossal difference in parenting styles was laid bare. I would rather spank a child than struggle with him and David was willing to let him freeze his rear end off as long as the child was not in distress. David and I had our first parent-on-parent argument and Matthew wore his snowsuit to his grandparents' house.

The discipline wars had begun.

High Noon

By Pam

Kids change the rules on you almost every day. It's hard to keep up. In my case, I either overthink or underestimate. Kae tells me all the time how much I over-analyze and worry too much. She also probably thinks I over-clean, over-childproof, over-bandage, and even over-cook. Well, overthinking wasn't what got me in trouble one hot day in July when Gracie was almost two years old. This time I underestimated my speedy little daughter's stubborn streak.

Gracie and I were splashing in her kiddie pool on the deck. We had been in the pool for about half an hour when her mood suddenly changed and she decided she no longer wanted to be outside. We climbed out of the little plastic pool and I dried her off with a towel. I then sat her at the picnic table under the umbrella and placed her sippy cup in front of her. While she happily sipped away at her juice, I turned away to hang the wet towels over the deck railing. That's when I heard the door open and close. *Slam!* I spun around and Gracie was no longer in her seat. She was now smiling at me from just inside the French doors.

She smiled and waved. I waved back and headed for the door. When I put my hand on the knob, the door wouldn't open. Gracie giggled. She had locked the door. I didn't have any keys with me. I was in my swimsuit on the deck; I never thought I'd need keys to sit in the kiddie pool in my own yard.

"Gracie, open the door for mommy please," I said.

Gracie giggled again and put her face up against the glass of the door. "Me locked it," she said, and put her hand to her mouth in a mock attempt at stifling a giggle.

"I know you locked it," I said, trying to be firm but calm, "but you locked mommy out of the house and that's not funny. Please open the door."

"No," came the response.

"Gracie, please open the door. Mommy needs to get into the house. It's not nice to lock me out."

"No."

"Gracie, you need to listen to mommy. Open the door, now," I said with the stern voice that Kae had been trying to teach me.

"No."

I put my face right up to the glass and continued in my low and intimidating Kae-type voice—the one she told me was much more effective than yelling. "Gracie, open the door, now! If you don't open the door now, you're going to be in trouble. Do as mommy tells you." My attempt at sounding quiet and intimidating didn't work. I was much better at panicky pleading. "Gracie, please open the door. It's very hot out here."

"Cool in here," she reported.

Great.

When my threats and begging didn't work, I thought I'd try to scare her by walking out of sight. If she thought I was leaving, perhaps she'd panic and open the door. I waved good-bye and walked off the deck and around the side of the house. After several minutes, I gave up and came back onto the deck. Gracie was now sitting right inside the door, calmly waiting for me. She had the power and she knew it. She had her middle-aged, out-of-shape mother stuck on the deck in her swimsuit without keys or a cell phone.

No amount of pleading or threats weakened Gracie one bit. Her two-year-old logic must've told her that she was already in big trouble, so why not simply go for broke. Maybe she thought that if she kept me out there long enough, I'd be so grateful to finally get in that I'd forego any punishment.

I remembered that years ago Scott had hidden a key somewhere in the backyard, but where? I thought I remembered him saying it was hanging on a nail under the deck. I walked off the deck and looked for a way underneath, but there was very little space between the deck and the ground. My husband had crawled under there countless times, but he had always been wearing coveralls. Many an air-conditioning repairman, exterminator, and cable guy had ventured under there as well, but they too had been dressed appropriately. None of them, as I recall, had attempted it in only a swimsuit. I knew there had to be at least one or two brown recluse or black widow spiders under there. Nope, that key could just sit there as far as I was concerned. Back up on the deck I went.

I looked through the bedroom window to see what time it was. So far, our stand-off had lasted over an hour. I was hot, mad, and very thirsty. Then I saw Gracie's sippy cup was still on the picnic table. I took a swig of the watered-down grape juice and noticed that Gracie's eyes seem to bug out a little. She may have been enjoying her little power trip, but she was mighty possessive of her Winnie the Pooh sippy cup.

Then I had another idea. I dragged Gracie's kiddie pool over to a shady part of the deck and stepped inside, partly to make her jealous, but also because I was so hot. I figured if I was going to spend the afternoon out in the heat, I might as well be comfortable. I sat down, hoisted the Winnie the Pooh sippy in a mock toast, and took a big swig. I splashed, laughed, and pretended to be having fun, as if it was perfectly normal for a woman in her late 40s to be drinking from a sippy cup while wedged into a kiddie pool.

Gracie stood up and put her hands on her hips. She was mad. It was getting to her. No one sits in her kiddie pool and drinks from her Winnie the Pooh sippy! I watched her as she stretched up to reach the doorknob. I heard the "click" of the lock and saw the door inch open.

"*My* sippy!" she scolded, and marched out the door to retrieve her rightful property.

"And you can have it back when you're finished in time-out," I announced. She was going to cool her heels for awhile.

It took two years before I would ever again risk stepping outside the house without a key. We've also moved the hidden key to a spot where one can easily retrieve it while wearing any type of swimwear.

Supermom Lost Her Spoon

By Kae

It was during one of the many shopping trips I took with my mother-in-law, Jackie, (shopping is the glue that binds all women together) that I realized there was a monumental difference between being a child's mother and being that child's grandmother.

One of our favorite places to shop was Marshall's. For those of you who don't have one in your town, it's a department store overflowing with brand-name clothing at discount prices. One step inside the front door and you will know you have entered a discount shopper's dream. Large colorful, pressboard signs hung above each section indicating the clothing type found below. Below these large signs were row after row after row of metal racks hung with clothing with no identifying markings except the small white discs that indicated where one size ended and the next size started.

In the early 1990s, Marshall's was famous for having brand-name clothing at as low as a quarter of the price of other retail stores. The savvy Marshall's shopper knew that both the large overhead signs and the small white markers were often wrong, though, so to be sure you missed nothing in your size, you had to peruse all garments on all racks in each and every section. It was truly a jungle for bargain hunters.

On this particular day, I carried Jessica into the store on my jutted-out left hip. Just inside the door was a row of gleaming metal carts. In one smooth move, I reached out with my right hand, grabbed the last shopping cart in the row by its red plastic handle, and gave the cart a quick snap of my wrist to make sure it was not attached to the cart it was cradled into. Once the cart was dislodged from the row and while it was still traveling backward toward me, I flipped the metal back of the child seat open and flopped the little red plastic seat cover down. In the same fluid movement, I bounced Jessica from my left hip, lifting her easily with my arm securely around her back, hand tucked under her under pit (as my children always called their underarms), and deposited her gently into the waiting seat with one leg on each side of the metal divider. This is a skill born of nine years of weekly practice. Jessica was the true beneficiary of all the bruises Matthew sported on his tiny little shins as I was trying to hone this particular skill.

Once Jessica was safely ensconced in the front seat of the shopping cart, Jackie said to me, "Why don't you go on and shop for yourself. Jessica and I will attack this side of the store." I rarely had the opportunity to shop without at least one of the three kids, and knowing that Jessica would be in more than capable hands, I wandered toward the other side of the store to shop in luxurious solitude.

When I became a mother, a strange phenomenon took place in my inner ear. It seems that somehow during childbirth, probably during the pushing phase when I had enough pressure built up in my head to run a torque wrench, I developed the ability to single out my child's vocal emissions from the rest of the auditory chaos surrounding me at any given time. As each of my children began to make sounds, I developed a kind of bionic hearing that could home in on them in just about any circumstance. I became so attuned to my children that, from our upstairs bedroom, I could actually hear my children downstairs roll over in their beds at night.

This bionic hearing is a great super skill to have if you want to make sure your child is not getting up during the night to raid the cookie jar. It is also wonderful to have as they get older so you can hear what they are muttering under their breaths as they walk away from you after being chastised. It is not such a great super skill when you are in a department store with the chance to spend some quality time by yourself.

I had just embarked on a new row of last season's winter wear when a certain distant whine tickled my bionic eardrum. My head snapped up like a drug sniffing dog catching the scent of cocaine at the airport. Quickly my eyes darted across the store. Like a laser beam, my eyes latched onto the face of my daughter. Her brows were knitted together, her arms folded across her tiny little chest, her chin stuck out stubbornly. Even to the untrained eye, this was a child on the verge of a shopping meltdown.

Without thinking, I took several steps toward the end of the aisle, intent on getting to Jessica before the siren went off. Then I stopped myself. Jackie had raised two wonderful children; surely she would be able to handle the situation without my interference. Mentally assured that Jackie had the situation well in hand, I returned to the racks and continued my shopping. A few minutes later, my bionic eardrum picked up the pre-tantrum whine again. Once again, my head snapped up from the garment I was looking at. Just as before, I scanned the store and quickly found Jessica's dark and sullen face.

It took every ounce of my self-restraint to keep from interfering in the grandmother-granddaughter dynamic. My mother-in-law and I were kindred spirits in the maternal world. Jackie is five feet tall, if you count the poof of hair on the top of her head. She has beautiful big brown eyes and an olive complexion that gives her a perpetual sun-kissed look. Jackie was a no-nonsense but fun loving mother. She was a legend in the Allen family for being a take-no-prisoners kind of mom. Legend has it that she wore a wooden spoon around her neck as a visual reminder of the spanking that spoon could dish out. The snap of her fingers in the doctor's office was like a sonic boom of discipline, rendering the offending child immediately compliant. One raised eyebrow was all it took to bring any naughty behavior to an abrupt end. Surely, I should not be worried that this maternal warrior would tolerate a public tantrum. I turned myself around and went right back to shopping.

Barely five minutes later, my bionic hearing picked up the distinct sound of my daughter's voice chanting, "I want down, I want down" perfectly synchronized with the banging of her sneaker-clad feet against the wire mesh of the shopping cart. That was the last straw for me. Grandmother-granddaughter dynamic or not, no child of mine would ever be allowed to act that way in public. I made a beeline toward the offending sound. Coming around the corner I saw my mother-in-law, the wooden-spoon-wearing, eyebrow-raising, finger-snapping warrior mother, reaching out to hand her squalling grandchild a piece of gum.

"No, no, no, mom! Don't give her gum for being bad," I said as I rushed up.

"Well, how else are you going to get her to quit fussing?" my mother-in-law asked me with the same big brown eyes as Jessica's.

"Like this," I said turning to Jessica. "Jessica Paige," I said sternly, with my eyebrows raised in the "you are about to get a spanking" expression. When I had Jessica's full attention, I raised my index finger sharply into the air in front of her face.

That's one.

It was communicated without me actually speaking a word. I raised my middle finger sharply next to my index finger.

That's two.

Then I followed with my ring finger.

That's three.

Once all three fingers were raised, Jessica inhaled a large gulp of air. She flicked her glaring gaze between me and Jackie. You could almost see the little calculator spinning in her head. What was the probability that she could go ahead and scream bloody murder in the middle of the store and not only be saved by her grandmother but also get the coveted piece of gum? On the other hand, what was the probability that her grandmother would not be able to save her and she would receive a spanking in the middle of the department store? Back and forth her big brown eyes darted as she weighed the options. Jackie and I stood there staring at this small child holding her breath and analyzing the situation. We were both holding our breaths as well, watching expectantly while the tiny little brown-eyed mathematician calculated her next step.

Jessica held the lung full of air for a brief moment longer, then simply exhaled. She didn't kick her feet again, she didn't make another sound. With an internal sigh of relief, I went back to the rack of clothing I had left when the crisis began. Grandmother and granddaughter continued on with their shopping as well. When our shopping adventure was finished, Jessica was rewarded for her "good" behavior with a piece of gum from her grandma's purse.

I was completely dumbfounded by my mother-in-law's reaction to Jessica's behavior that day. It wasn't until years later that I realized the reason we are such strict and unbending mothers is because everything our child grows up to be is on our shoulders. We are responsible for making sure that our children grow up to be happy, healthy, loving, productive members of society. There is no such pressure on grandmothers. The grandmother has already done her duty for the universe. Now she can sit back and enjoy the fruits of her labor—grandchildren!

Little Criminals

By Pam

I hate grocery shopping. I hated it long before I was a mother and had to contend with keeping my kids entertained while attempting to get through my shopping list. I don't even like shopping for clothes all that much. I truly believe that somehow, I was not given the shopping gene so many other women happily possess. As a result, I'm not a very savvy shopper. I'm basically your grab-and-go kind of consumer. So I miss a lot of bargains and I don't even attempt to comparison shop. I tell you this because it explains why I have returned home with the oddest of items. Thanks to the sticky fingers of Gracie and Jack, I have hastily placed things on the cashier's conveyor belt that I never intended to buy. When one is trying to prevent a double toddler meltdown at the checkout, one doesn't always scrutinize what's getting scanned and bagged.

I like to think my two kids are little angels who will grow up to be hardworking, productive members of society. The truth is, though, their life of crime has already begun. In fact, I'll bet there are a number of mothers out there who have acquired odd and unique objects due to the sticky fingers of their toddlers.

It started out with small, seemingly innocent objects like cans of olives (I hate olives) and packages of shoelaces. As my kids grew a bit older and wiser, however, they began to recognize the objects they wanted and started picking and choosing their loot more care-fully. I'm convinced they even managed to work out a bait-and-switch scheme where one would distract me with the beginnings of a meltdown while the other leaned over and snatched boxes of cookies or bags of candy off the shelves.

When Jack became a toddler, my kids' life of crime really went into high gear. Before that, all items tossed into the shopping cart were paid for by me, unless I happened to realize at the last minute that I had no use for three jars of mayonnaise. Once Jack was old enough not to have to sit in the seat of the shopping cart, I lost a very important visual advantage. Both kids wanted to sit in the "race cart" grocery shopping cart. It consisted of a two-seater car attached to the front end of the ordinary grocery cart. The race cart sits low in front, so as the driver of the cart, I couldn't really see what was happening down there.

I was, of course, a careful mom and made sure my kids were strapped in and that all arms and legs were kept inside for the most part. But kids have radar, as you know, and they wait for the moment when you're reading the ingredients on a label or reaching up for a product high on the top shelf. That's when they strike with lightning speed to stock up on those much-needed items such as dog treats (we didn't have a dog at the time) and denture cleaner (I still have my own teeth). I assume my kids chose these items because of the packaging—a happy dog on one label and a big smiley face on the other.

For many reasons (not the least of which was their budding shoplifting career), I tried to do my grocery shopping while they were either at preschool or late at night after they were in bed. There were times, however, when it was inevitable that Butch Cassidy and the Sundance Kid had to accompany me to the grocery store. Before we entered the store, I would kneel down, look them directly in the eyes, and give them the standard lecture on how the items in the store were not just theirs for the taking and that it was dishonest to put something in the cart that we had no intention of paying for. My kids looked back at me with the most innocent expressions and nodded in agreement, telling me they understood the concept. We would then walk hand-in-hand into the store, pick out our "race cart," and proceed to the produce aisle. Even though my children promised me they would keep their fingers off the merchandise, for the next few visits I had them step out of the cart before we left the checkout area. When no contraband was discovered, I felt confident that I had rehabilitated my little criminals.

Shopping with my children became a joy. I happily shopped while my two kids chattered away in their little race cart. Fellow shoppers would even periodically tell me how well-mannered my children were in public. I was definitely a proud mom. I had mastered one of the most difficult tasks one can do with young children—shop.

One Saturday, while walking out of the store with my two angelic children in their favorite positions in their race cart, I noticed several people pointing to my kids and smiling. My kids are extremely cute (yes, I know your kids are cute too, but this is *my* book), and it wasn't at all unusual for people to stop and comment on their looks. So it didn't strike me as odd that several people were pointing at my kids. As we crossed the parking lot, however, I saw that a couple of people were covering their mouths and giggling. *Oh great,* I thought, *Jack is probably picking his nose again.* I stopped the cart and bent down to get a close look at which child had a finger up their nose. What I saw, though, was not nose-picking at all. It appeared that my children's tendency for shoplifting had not been eradicated after all. In their hands was a box of tampons. That was not the worst of it. Gracie and Jack had unwrapped a few of the tampons and wedged them in their ears. The rest of them were being casually tossed out of the cart, one by one. I looked back at the entrance to the store and saw a trail of tampons strewn across the pavement like a demented version of Hansel and Gretel's breadcrumbs.

I felt my cheeks turn bright red as I spun the shopping cart around to retrieve the tampons. I then raced to the car, pulled my kids out of their getaway vehicle, and strapped them into their car seats with no plans of ever returning to this particular store again.

Fortunately, it only took a few more of those Serious Mommy Talks to convince my children to stay on the right side of the law. I'm also very grateful that my children weren't curious enough to ask what those objects were that they stuck in their ears. They were content to refer to them as their "alien ears." I wasn't ready to sit my kids down yet and have the talk about menstruation and reproduction. One crisis was enough.

Chapter 7

Clean-Up on Aisle Four

Supply and Demand

By Kae

Nursing your child is one of the most natural acts a mother can perform. By the time my second child was born, life had provided me with a wonderful husband and a stable home life. I was going to be a good mother and nurse my child. I read the *All the Goofy Advice About Nursing* books. There were several items of importance that seemed to have been left out of the ones I purchased, though. I also felt betrayed by all the women who came before me in the nursing hall of fame who had led me down the rosy path to believe nursing was a wonderful natural bonding experience for mother and child.

For example, no one really tells you up front that your breasts will become throbbing masses of engorged flesh. No one tells you that you will spend the next year wearing the upper-body equivalent of a maxi pad in your bra. No one tells you that your breasts will be treated like a fast food take-out window at noon. No one ever tells you that a ravenous infant can create more suction than most industrial-grade vacuum cleaners. No one ever tells you that by the time you are finished nursing, your breasts will bear no resemblance to the breasts you had going into this little adventure. All the unsuspecting first-time nursing mother sees is the romanticized version on the covers of the *All the Goofy Advice About Nursing* books, which show a happy woman wearing a beautiful dressing gown, gazing lovingly at the face of a perfect little child suckling gently on her breast.

Reality set in for me the day after Christina was born. I went to sleep with my standard, fairly small breasts and woke up with jugs the size of over-inflated footballs. I couldn't move my arms or shoulders. My breasts were on fire and trying to consume the entire top half of my body. When I called the nurse, she just laughed and said, "Oh, good. Your milk has come in." Good lord! *My milk has come in.* It was more like my breasts had acquired a dairy farm overnight and we were open for business.

The nurse brought Christina over to me and said, "Now hon, some babies just don't know how to suck right off, so don't get discouraged if she doesn't nurse the first time. We can bring you a pump to relieve your breasts and you can try again next time." At this point anything that would provide relief to my aching upper body was okey-dokey with me. All I cared about was deflating the footballs on my chest so I could take full breaths again.

Childbirth in and of itself can be quite a humiliating experience. First, you have your nether regions splayed out for everyone in the room to see— even yourself if you have the guts to look in the mirror they so politely set up so that you, too, can get a bird's-eye view of the carnage. Christina was born in a teaching hospital, so we had at least five people in the room not related to the child being born. Later, the fun really began when the doctor brought all the students along for his daily rounds. By the time I left, everyone on staff at the hospital—including the janitor, I think—had gotten a peek at my nether regions.

Even with all of this attention, nothing prepared me for the nurse reaching down and pulling my breast out of my nightgown and then flicking my nipple to see if she could get the baby to latch on. In all the years that have past, I have never figured out exactly what that woman was trying to do. It's all well and good that she was a lactation nurse and saw hundreds of women's breasts every year. But this was *my* breast and she needed to keep her lactation nurse hands and flicker to herself.

After about 10 seconds of this less-than-acceptable attention from Nurse Flicker, I said, "Maybe I could just give it a try and call you back if I have any problems." Nurse Flicker left the room less than thrilled but sure she would be back to help me in a few minutes when Christina grew tired of waiting for her meal.

When it came to eating, though, Christina's Allen ancestry made itself known. David's grandmother was always somewhat distressed that Matthew was a skinny little string bean and constantly used to tell him, "Eat, you'll get big." Grandma Allen was a strong, stout woman with a formidable constitution. When Christina was born with cheeks so round she couldn't get her eyes open and three rolls of fat on her little thighs, Grandma Allen was delighted. Here was good Allen stock.

True to her heritage, Christina needed no prodding. She latched right on and started nursing greedily—and nosily. I began to giggle. This little ruddy-faced baby latched to my breast was moaning delightedly with each mouthful of milk, her little legs kicking like crazy.

Christina's first near-miss on a medical emergency was the day we were going to bring her home from the hospital. David had come to the hospital to bring us home, but I was in the middle of nursing Christina when he arrived. David sat in a chair and we discussed all the things we hadn't had time to discuss because I was in the hospital and he was home with Matthew. When Christina was finished eating, I set her up for the post-luncheon burping. One little pat on the back and the child spewed a stream of recycled mother's milk five feet across the room. Christina's little baby face was frozen with her eyes wide and her mouth making a perfect little O. It seemed like the shear force of expelling the milk from her stomach had created a vacuum that was now pulling the air out of the child. She began to turn slightly blue. "Get the nurse," I said to David, but he was already halfway out the door. I put Christina on my lap and gave her back a firm pat. Something in that pat must have broken the vacuum seal, because she inhaled sharply and began to wail. Hearing the screaming, David came back in the door. All was fine. It scared the poop out of both of us, but no harm was done—except to the floor.

Christina continued to wail. At first I thought she was scared and would calm down with some bouncing, swaying, and cooing on my part. I was wrong. She wasn't scared at all. She was ticked off that her lunch had escaped and she wanted it back. As a last resort, I pulled out my breast and offered it to her. To my surprise, she took the breast greedily and nursed a full meal. When she was done, I tentatively set her up for the after-luncheon burp. This time we were treated to nothing more than a resounding belch that any man would be proud to produce.

We took our precious daughter home and began our life as a family of four. Christina continued to projectile vomit after the majority of her feedings, then demand another full feeding that always stayed down just fine. At her two-week checkup I mentioned this to her doctor. He said it wasn't uncommon for a child to be born with what he referred to as "immature bowel syndrome." Basically, the valve between her esophagus and her stomach was not yet closing properly. He assured me this would eventually correct itself. There was nothing for us to do or worry about.

But with Christina, the problem wasn't just immature bowel syndrome. It was also gluttony. Christina loved to eat and delighted in partaking of her daily meals in large, moaning gulps. Take the fact that the child ate twice what she probably should be eating, packing her little tummy to literally the bursting point, and couple it with a leaky valve between the holding tank and the outside air, and you have the perfect recipe for projectile vomiting.

One other important thing no one told me was that when your milk lets down, it can spray out of your nipples with enough force to take paint off cement. The first time I experienced this was a few days after I brought Christina home from the hospital. By then, her cycle of nursing, vomiting, then nursing again had already been established. It was apparent that I was nursing twins in the same body. My breasts stayed full and swollen. I called the lactation nurse at my doctor's office and she told me I could pump the remainder of the milk from my breasts and save it in the freezer for times when I would not be able to nurse the baby.

What the lactation nurse neglected to tell me was that the more milk you remove from your breasts, the more they make. It is a perfect supply and demand system. Your child initiates a demand and your body supplies it in full—sometimes with a little extra to spare. The long and the short of it is that by both nursing and pumping, my breasts had received an order to supply the milk for a small third world nation. I was over-engorged again within days and just as sore and swollen as ever.

Another unwitting consequence of putting in such a large demand order was that the build-up of milk with only the narrow outlet of my nipples created a tremendous amount of pressure. The first time this happened, Christina had latched on and took her first long pull on the nectar of life. This signaled the breast that it was time to let the milk down, and down it came in a torrent. Christina's eyes flew open wide and she began to sputter and choke as milk began escaping from her nostrils. Obviously, this was not normal, so I pulled her off my breast and the milk sprayed like an untended fire hose. I grabbed the burping towel and put it over my breast in an attempt to save Christina from being flogged and/or drowned by her daily meal. After a few minutes, the pressure decreased enough that Christina could latch back on without fear of drowning. Christina nursed, projectile vomited, then nursed again. Finally fat and happy, she slid back into the blissful sleep that only babies can achieve.

I went to the bathroom to clean up and put on clean clothes, just as I did after every feeding. When I pulled my bra off, milk was literally dripping from the cups. I had soaked through not only the two nursing pads, but also the fabric of the bra itself. Something had to give. This was too much to have to put up with every time I fed my baby!

The next feeding, I took my top off completely, let Christina latch onto one nipple, and held the battery-powered breast pump over the unoccupied breast. Christina took her first slurp and the milk let down with the same force as before. Christina, as before, became wide-eyed and started sputtering and choking. Once again, milk leaked out from her nostrils. But I was prepared this time. I had a thick towel on my shoulder so all I had to do was drop it down over my breast to protect Christina. I watched in amazement as the breast pump bottle rapidly filled from one ounce to two to three.

As soon as my nipples were safe to approach again, I let Christina resume her feeding. She fed on one side while I pumped the other, then she projectile vomited on my chest. As with every feeding since we had come home, I washed my chest with the washcloth I had ready at hand and then finished nursing Christina on the breast I had been pumping. Meanwhile, I continued to pump the breast that Christina had first nursed from. Christina was fat and happy after her feeding. I was relieved and delighted to have found an answer to the milk over-production issue.

Freedom of Expression

By Pam

When it came to being in her crib, there were two distinct sides to Gracie. During the day, her naps were wonderful and uneventful. She'd have her lunch, a diaper change, and then off to dreamland she'd go. When it was time to wake up, I'd hear her softly cooing through the baby monitor. Most times she'd stay dry during her nap, or at the very least, her diaper would be slightly wet.

At night, we'd go through the typical routine of dinner, bath, PJs, and a bedtime story. This was such a wonderful time for me because I loved to snuggle with my freshly bathed baby. She had that wonderfully clean baby scent and she felt so soft and precious. But when Gracie turned one, I became initiated into the experience every mother dreads but must go through—when baby removes her own diaper. For some mothers, the worst that happens is that baby happily stands buck naked in the crib, pleased as punch at her new ability to show off her private parts. For other mothers (and I am in this latter category), the diaper removal comes with a very unpleasant side effect—poop has been set free.

Because I was one of those mothers who lived in fear of any type of object in the crib being a potential hazard for my child, Gracie slept without a blanket. To keep her warm, I used one piece, footed, snap or zipper pajamas. It was late at night and I was about to walk into Gracie's room to check on her before I went to bed. The smell hit me long before my hand even touched the doorknob. I cracked open the door and the overwhelming stench filled my nostrils. As my eyes adjusted to the low light, I saw that my daughter had decorated her crib, the wall, and herself with poop. She had managed to unsnap her pajamas, detach the diaper closure, and was alone with her palette of poop to express her creativity.

I used to be a veterinary technician, so I have a pretty strong stomach for foul-smelling things. I saw, smelled, and cleaned plenty of poop during that time. Having it on my furniture, walls, and child, however, took my iron stomach by surprise. I ran to the bathroom and heaved into the toilet. Once my stomach was emptied of its contents, I prepared myself for Operation Poop Removal.

"Scott!" I yelled back over my shoulder as I returned to the scene of the crime. Scott was in another part of the house watching a football game.

I scooped up my poop-covered baby and headed back to the bathroom. Scott came around the corner, took one look at Gracie, and put his hand over his mouth. I stepped to the side just in case he needed a clear path to the toilet.

"Gracie removed her diaper and spread poop all over her crib and the walls. I'm going to put her in the tub. Will you strip the crib and start washing the walls?"

Scott hesitantly walked into the bedroom and then quickly returned. "I don't think I can. It smells too bad."

I rolled my eyes. "Come on," I said. "Just go in there, get nauseated, come vomit in the toilet, and then you'll be fine."

Scott looked at me in horror.

"Oh, forget it," I said. "I'll do it myself." My husband can handle a lot of things and has relatively little fear, but toss a little baby poop on the wall and he's out the door.

I bathed Gracie and then handed my now-sweet-smelling child over to Scott so I could tackle her bedroom. I gathered my bucket, cleanser, clean sheets, rubber gloves, and one of my husband's dust masks. I stripped off my pajamas and cleaned her room in my pink underpants, yellow rubber gloves, and a blue dust mask.

This became my initiation into being able to handle whatever foul-smelling, foul-looking, yucky stuff came out of my children.

After that night, nothing affected me. I have since caught projectile vomit in my bare hands to prevent it from reaching my carpet, deftly handled a diarrhea-soaked child during many a public outing, been handed a pile of nose buggers, and have even reached into a dirty toilet bare-handed to retrieve whatever valuable object one of my children decided to toss in there to keep their poop company during its trip down the pipes.

Regardless of my ability to handle poop catastrophes, I had to find a way to prevent my daughter from getting out of her diaper. I went the obvious route: duct tape.

The following night I placed a roll of duct tape on her changing table next to her powder and diaper rash ointment. After closing the Velcro on her diaper, I placed a piece of duct tape over each closure for extra insurance.

Duct tape isn't as strong as one is lead to believe. When I went in to check on my daughter, she was once again naked and had recreated her poop mural on the wall. To this day I don't know how my little baby managed to unfasten the duct tape, but the proof—both visual and olfactory—was right in front of me. Off came my clothes again and out came the rubber gloves, bucket, cleanser, and another of Scott's dust masks.

Okay, I thought, *maybe I've been going at this the wrong way. Instead of concentrating on her diaper, I should concentrate on securing her pajamas better.* The next morning I went to the store and bought diaper pins. My plan was to pin the pajama zipper closed, but when I actually took the pin out of the package, I couldn't do that to my baby. Now, I know they used to use those barbaric diaper pins to hold cloth diapers closed, but there was no way I was putting such a sharp object near my baby. And, based on her duct tape removal strength, I was convinced she'd be able to open the pin herself anyway. I needed another plan. I looked at her pajamas and came up with a solution.

I got my scissors and cut the feet off the pajamas. Then I put the pajamas on her backward so they fastened up the back. I put socks on her feet to keep her warm and then held her up to inspect my work. Gracie just looked at me with a smile that seemed to say she welcomed the challenge.

"Hopefully, you won't remember this, kid," I whispered to her. At this point, there were many things I was hoping my daughter wouldn't remember.

That night I put Gracie to bed and then periodically peeked in to see if she had managed to pull a Houdini and get out of her pajamas. She seemed to quickly realize it was not worth the effort, and from that day on, no longer needed to decorate with poop.

She wore her pajamas backward for several more months, though, just in case.

Lactose Intolerance

By Kae

My first child was lactose intolerant. I didn't even know what lactose was, much less that one could be intolerant of it. The first several months of Matthew's life on this planet were consumed with me trying to figure out how to keep what he was putting into his diapers inside the diaper and off of me. Luckily, my grandmother informed me that "everything that comes out of a baby's body is good for your complexion." If this was true, I was going to be peaches and cream.

The evolution of the diaper is a remarkable story. By definition, a diaper is a "garment consisting of a folded cloth drawn up between the legs and fastened at the waist; worn by infants to catch excrement." The British call it a "nappy"; cute as that is, it's still an excrement catcher. Originally, diapers were made of folded pieces of cloth that were fastened at the waist with large "safety" pins. I don't know who thought that putting a slim piece of stiff wire sharp enough to easily pierce multiple layers of cotton batting around the waist of tender-fleshed little babies was a good idea.

In 1950, a woman named Marion Donovan invented the first disposable diaper by stuffing a shower curtain with absorbent material. Her invention was dubbed the Boater. Believe it or not, the men who ran the world in the 1950s didn't think there was a market for such a product. Mrs. Donovan, undeterred by men who in the 1950s probably wouldn't know the input end of the baby from the output end, decided to market the product herself. Mrs. Donovan eventually sold her interest in the product for one million dollars. Not bad bling for an excrement catcher.

By the time I arrived on the diaper scene in the early 1980s, there were several brands of disposable diapers available. Compared to today, the construction of these diapers was still quite rudimentary. There were limited size options, ranging from newborn to whatever poundage was deemed too heavy to poop your pants. My newborn son, with legs the circumference of the big pencils used by kindergarten children to write their first letters, was expected to fill the same opening that the future sumo wrestlers of the world filled. There were no recloseable tabs so you could peek to see if there really was a boom-boom or just a pre-boom-boom warning flare. There were no elastic bands around the legs to keep the seal tight around the thighs, eliminating that always inconvenient and often embarrassing excrement escapeage.

No indicator let you know when the child was wet. We of the dark ages of disposable diapers had to use the weigh-the-baby technique. This involved holding the baby's bottom in one hand and gently tossing up and down, sort of like testing a melon in the grocery store. If the weight seemed off or the drop into the hand produced a squishy sensation, time for a diaper change. Of course, this technique occasionally rewarded the unsuspecting parent with excrement escapeage as the weight of the baby's bottom pressed firmly against the parent's palm, overwhelming the inadequately fitting leg holes.

There are so many times that caring for a child puts the parents in a situation that is just not covered in the *How to Be a Stellar Parent Handbook*. One such incident happened to me about five months into motherhood.

I had been toying with the idea of selling my house and buying a new one. I had several houses lined up to see with the realtor this particular beautiful early summer day. I was always the type of parent who brought my child with me just about everywhere. I birthed him and he became a part of my daily life. Plus, I was a single mother back then. Since I had to bring the baby, car seat, and diaper bag, I decided it would be easier to meet the realtor at each location rather than transferring all the baby paraphernalia from my car to hers. Also, as I had quickly learned, you must always have a viable escape route from every situation when you have an infant in tow. There is no guarantee that some baby crisis will not call for an immediate retreat.

We started out at midmorning, just after Matthew's morning nap and a quick bottle. This schedule ensured there would be at least two hours of happy baby time forthcoming. I packed the immediately necessary items into the diaper bag: three premixed bottles of formula, 12 diapers (remember, my child had lactose issues), two full changes of clothes, two extra pairs of shorts, a large box of premoistened baby wipes, a portable changing pad, diaper rash cream, plastic bags for dirty disposals, two extra bibs (not counting the one around his neck—he was a drooler), iced teething rings, plastic zoo animals, and various car-appropriate toys.

I met the realtor at the first of four houses we planned to tour, pulled the child in his car seat out of the car, and proceeded to carry both on my left hip with a diaper bag weighing approximately 50 pounds slung over my right shoulder. Here I have to tell you that I am a small woman. I stand just over five-foot-three and at the time weighed all of 100 pounds when wet. Luckily, I had prominent hip bones and if I jutted my hip out just right, the car seat sat on it as on a shelf. Having the diaper bag worked as a counterweight, which kept me from listing precariously to the left. After two hours of toting baby and bag, struggling in and out of the car over and over, we finally arrived at the last house on the list. It was a 1950 beach-type house in a great neighborhood with lots of small children, as evidenced by the "Slow Children at Play" sign and the various trikes, bikes, balls, and wading pools scattered on the lawns. This could be the place.

The front door opened into a large living-dining room area with a kitchen across the dining area to the left and two bedrooms with a bath between across the living area to the right. The floor plan was so open that you could see all the living area and kitchen from anywhere in the common areas. This would be the perfect place to raise a toddler. Since the space was so open and the house was vacant, I decided it would be okay if I left the baby in the car seat with diaper bag in attendance in the middle of the living room floor while I spent the five minutes necessary to view the remainder of the little house.

"This house is exactly what I'm looking for. The bedrooms are small but big enough and the bath is older but in good shape," I was telling the realtor as we came out of the small hallway back into the living area, "but it sort of has a strange smell, don't you think?"

"No, I don't smell a thing," she said to me. All the while her eyes were casting about frantically trying to locate the offensive odor.

"Let me make sure we got all the lights," she said as she headed back down the small hallway toward the bathroom. I was sure she was checking the plumbing.

I picked up the car seat and diaper bag and was about to meet the realtor in the doorway when I noticed my perfectly content little man had a very strained look on his face. In a flash, I identified the offensive smell.

"Oh, look at the time. I have to run before the baby's next feeding," I said as I made a beeline for the front door. "I'll think about the house and call you later," I added as I quickly shut the door behind me. I hightailed it to the car and lickety-split had the car seat buckled in, diaper bag stowed in the passenger seat, and car in gear headed for home.

I put the windows down and made sure to keep the speedometer at 40 whenever possible to aid in the circulation of the fresh air from outside the car. At the next stoplight I turned in my seat to check the status of the disaster that was brewing. To my dismay, I saw that Matthew was literally filling his car seat with his lactose intolerance. There he sat, his face all red and pinched. The car seat was filling quickly and he showed no outward sign of being finished.

Frantically, my mind started rapid-firing questions of logistics. What is the capacity of this particular infant seat? I don't think there's a government rating system in place for excrement. Molded plastic—does that mean no holes or seams? At what point did the shoulder strap slots come into play? (Don't even think about the buckle attachment!) Was the cloth liner plastic-lined on the back? (Yes, yes, I think so, maybe.) Would this ruin the leather car seat?

Could this one event leave a lasting odor in the car, making it impossible to drive with the windows up? What if it got down into the crack of the seat? How do you get that out? Does the seat unhinge or something? Exactly how much had I fed this child and why was it all coming out at one time? Could this be natural? Maybe he'd perforated something and this was a more serious health crisis. Should we go to the ER instead of the house? One thing was very, very clear: We were in deep poop.

Finally, I pulled into the driveway and parked the car, being careful not to park on the incline but to pull up almost touching the garage door where the driveway was flat. For a young single mother, a Nissan 300z was the bomb. For a woman with a child floating in a car seat filled to the brim with lactose intolerance, the two-door sportscar was a nightmare.

I left the driver's door open for extra ventilation and walked around to the passenger side where the baby was riding in the back seat. I opened the door and slid the front seat as far forward as the little metal track would allow and then tipped the front seat forward. This gave me the largest aperture possible from which to extract the toxic yet delicate on so many levels mess from my back seat. With the portal prepared, I proceeded to walk several slow circles around the car peering in all the windows, taking in the scene from all vantage points. This was not a time for haste. Clear and calm, that was what was called for. I pulled large quantities of fresh air through my nose and exhaled to the count of five through my mouth, willing myself to hold steady. I cast a glance up and down the street, hoping maybe one of my neighbors would be outside watering the grass or walking the dog and would possibly be able to help me. But not today.

Screwing my courage to the sticking place, I finally crawled in the back seat from the driver's side. Trick number one was to remove the seat belt strap that held the car seat in place without running the strap through the muck, which was perilously close to the bottom edge. Since the strap automatically recoiled into a mechanism in the seat, it was imperative for it to come out unscathed. With a firm grasp on the strap where it met the buckle, I quickly hit the release button while lifting the belt straight up and to the left, out of harm's way, then let it gently retract.

I crawled out of the car on the passenger side, bent at the waist, and lifted the car seat off the seat. Keeping my arms, shoulders, and hips at precisely the same level, I carefully swung the back of the car seat toward the door and, like a forklift, backed straight out of the car, being ever so careful not to whack the car seat on the back of the seat or the door frame. This was a huge deal for me. I am the woman who once hit my hand so hard between the car seat and the door frame of the car that I knocked the diamond out of my engagement ring. But that's another story.

With the extraction complete and no spillage in the car, I put the baby and the car seat in the grass and dropped down on the ground beside them. I asked my son exactly what he was thinking, but he didn't answer. I also asked him if he had any brilliant ideas on how to clean this up. He still didn't answer. He didn't start talking for another six months and we just couldn't wait that long. During his protracted silence, I weighed my options.

I could pull the child out and wrap him in a towel, carry him quickly though the house with its lovely beige carpeting to the bathroom, but I couldn't put him in the bathtub because there is no way that much lactose intolerance would be good for the drainpipes. I could also rinse him in the toilet first like a dirty cloth diaper, but that seemed somewhat irresponsible. I could call my mom at work and see if she could come home and handle this. Surely she would know what to do with this mess. I could carefully remove Matthew from the car seat right here, take off his clothes, and then throw everything but the naked baby in the garbage can.

During the time it took me to weigh my options, my child decided that his situation was amazingly similar to bath time in the kitchen sink—you know, where you make the bubbles and the baby spends countless minutes slapping at the water and giggling his little head off. So there he was, just slapping and giggling and sending lactose intolerance everywhere.

Sitting in the grass being splattered with lactose intolerance, the solution came to me in a flash of brilliance. I went around to the side of the house and picked up the garden hose, stretched it out along the grass to where the disaster zone was, and turned on the spray. Of course, you can't just turn the sprayer nozzle on full blast as if you're hosing out a horse stall. It took a few seconds to test the various types of spray patterns to select the perfect one for the job. The mist setting just didn't have the force needed, while the stream would be effective but not exactly baby friendly. Finally I settled on half pressure. This requires a delicate touch. If you go about this the wrong way, there's a good chance you will give your child a phobia of garden hoses and outdoor bathing.

I guess it would have been a little more discreet if I had taken Matthew and the car seat around to the side of the house instead of putting on our little show out in the front yard, 15 feet from the street, when all my neighbors were streaming in from work. But who thinks of these things during a crisis? And besides, 10 minutes ago when I was hoping to get some well-meaning neighborly help, there was no one in sight.

With garden hose in hand and sprayer regulated to a soft but forceful enough stream as to be effective against the quickly cementing lactose intolerance, I approached the car seat wishing I was wearing those lovely yellow gloves my grandma keeps under the sink in her kitchen. I could have gone into the house and looked to see if I had a pair of lovely yellow gloves under my own kitchen sink, but it seemed to me that it would be highly inappropriate to leave my child strapped in his car seat full of lactose intolerance in the middle of the front yard unattended. In retrospect, I don't think anyone would have taken him under the circumstances.

Assessing the situation, I realized that the seat was full above the buckle. With no yellow gloves, I wasn't about to stick my hand in there to undo the buckle and retrieve the child. Not to mention, once I did get him out, what would I do with him? Lay him in the grass wet and filthy until I get the rest cleared up?

Okay, so the child and the car seat had to remain one unit until the majority of the mess was taken care of. At first it seemed the easiest way to wash out the seat was to run the spray in the short side and let the water build up in the seat. Once the hardening mass was softened, it would easily slide out the long gentle slope down the driveway and, hopefully, into the gutter. I double-checked that the shoulder straps holding Matthew in his seat were on securely and that he wasn't going to flop out or dangle dangerously by his neck when I tipped the car seat forward or back or side to side.

I moved the car seat onto the concrete driveway and began filling the seat with water, being careful not to get any in the baby's face and making sure it didn't get above his neck. I held the seat with one hand and the hose with the other, and gently tipped the car seat backward; the yuck starting running out just as I had envisioned. I continued to run the water down the back of the car seat between the plastic back and the cloth liner, letting it sluice out of the seat and down the driveway. The plan was working perfectly. The baby was kicking his legs and flapping his little arms, making his happy baby sounds, when I realized his face had turned beet red. So, okay, I didn't take into account that my cleaning method would involve Matthew being tipped backwards and upside down.

Quickly, I set the car seat flat on the ground again and filled it with water, playing the bath time slap-the-water game to make sure Matthew was okay. He was fine—still kicking and flapping. So I tipped the car seat forward, this time making sure his head stayed in the full upright position. When the majority of lactose intolerance was out of the seat, down the driveway, and into the sewer grate by the mailbox, the time had come to address the baby.

Still in the seat, I began to undress my little man. First off with the shirt, which, unfortunately had to come up over his head. Since the shirt was not the most sanitary item, I thought rolling it up from the bottom inside out would enable me to quickly pass it over his head and not spread too much muck on Matthew. This would have worked brilliantly, except that the lack of elastic around the waist band of his rudimentary disposable diaper allowed for a certain amount of, shall we say, upward flow. This came to my attention after I had whipped the shirt over his head and left a fresh swath of lactose intolerance up the back of the head and into the hair on top. Since it wasn't on his face, I just moved on to his pants. I took the Band-Aid approach: yank them quickly and then deal with the aftermath.

Now I had a naked, filthy baby boy, still flapping his arms happy as a clam, sitting in a half-ruined car seat on my front lawn. I took

Clean-Up on Aisle Four

the garden hose and gently washed the yuck from his hair and body until the water ran clean and clear. We got behind his ears, under his "underpits" (as my kids call the underarms), in the small of the back, behind the knees, and between the toes.

The clothes and the cloth liner of the car seat ended up in the garbage can. The car seat sat in ammonia mixed with water in the utility sink in the garage for two days before I would use it again. The grass beside the driveway grew twice as fast that summer. I took the naked baby into the house and we had a real bath in the kitchen sink with tons of bubbles and lots of slapping and giggling.

My son is grown now. I have had many years to watch for any signs of phobias to garden hoses or outdoor bathing and have seen none. He won't go on roller coasters, though.

Pet Supplies

By Pam

My husband understands and accepts that I'm your basic clean freak and germophobe. Before we had kids, I patrolled our home to make sure all dust bunnies were found and eliminated, and all surfaces were scrubbed or polished daily. When we brought Gracie home, I was determined to keep all dirt and germs at bay. After all, I now had a precious, vulnerable little being to protect.

One area of cleanliness that was frustrating me was the changing pad I used for Gracie. I bought the typical vinyl-covered pad and a few terry cloth washable covers. No matter how hard I tried to coordinate keeping Gracie's poopy bottom elevated while I wiped and dried her, I always managed to get something on the terry cloth cover. It also seemed that whenever I unfastened the diaper, Gracie felt the need to unleash a stream of pee into the air. I had watched other mothers practically suspend their babies in midair, wipe the bulk of the poop with a clean portion of the old diaper, fold the dirty diaper, deposit it in the diaper pail, clean the baby's bottom, attach a clean diaper and, voilá, not a speck of powder or a droplet of poop landed anywhere other than where it was assigned. As for me, poop, pee, and diaper rash cream tended to end up all over the terry cover of the changing pad. This meant it had to be stripped and the cover washed immediately.

My options were to buy terry cloth covers in bulk or do laundry several times a day. I just couldn't figure out how other mothers were managing it. Surely I wasn't the only OCD mother on the planet.

One morning while I was at the pet supply store to get a box of cat litter, I walked by a display for trial-size boxes of disposable puppy wee wee pads. The pads consisted of a thin, waterproof plastic sheet topped with a layer of absorbent material. *Hmmm,* I thought, *do I dare buy these for Gracie?* No way! I pushed my shopping cart on toward the cat litter.

"Well, it's worth a try, isn't it?" I asked my infant daughter, who was busily eyeing the brightly colored dog toys on display. "I mean, it's just an absorbent pad, right? It could be our little secret, okay?"

After getting the cat litter, I spun the shopping cart around and headed back toward the wee wee pad display. *It will just be an experiment,* I told myself. *No one has to know.* I casually dropped one of the trial-size boxes into my cart and headed toward the checkout.

The puppy wee wee pads worked like a charm. The disposable pad covered the vinyl changing pad, and whenever any pee or poop landed on it, I just crumpled it up, tossed it in the trash, and whipped out a clean pad. Gracie didn't seem to mind at all and no one ever asked me what the unusual covering was.

When my trial-size supply ran out, I happily went back to the pet supply store to stock up on more puppy wee wee pads. They had several sizes, and I chose the most economical jumbo box. When I got to the checkout counter with my jumbo box of puppy wee wee pads, I was feeling pretty pleased with myself. I had managed to find a practical solution to a frustrating problem. I was feeling like Mighty Imaginative Mommy. I was even beginning to feel as if I shouldn't be keeping this secret of the puppy wee wee pads to myself. There were probably many mothers out there who would appreciate a way to keep the changing pad cleaner. As I handed my money to the cashier, I made the decision that I would spread my secret to help others.

"Wow, that's a big box of pads," the cashier said. "How many puppies do you have?"

"None," I answered with a smile, "they're for my daughter."

The cashier looked at me in horror with her mouth agape. She then quickly handed me my change and hurried on to the next customer in line before I could explain my brilliant idea.

I decided that my puppy wee wee pad revelation would remain my secret a little longer. Maybe the world just wasn't ready for Mighty Imaginative Mommy.

Chapter 8

A Laugh a Day Keeps the Therapist Away

Pirate Sofa

By Kae

It had been raining for days and the backyard was saturated. The kids had been inside for a couple of days, though, so we all went out anyway. But after a few minutes it became clear that any further time spent outside would be a disaster in the laundry department. On top of that, a huge black cloud was building behind our house, so I quickly gathered the troops and retreated to the safety of our humble abode.

I opened the back door and Matthew and Christina climbed the steps to our mud porch. "Make sure to take off your muddy shoes at the top of the steps," I said as I carried Jessica on my hip into the house. No sooner had the words come out of my mouth than a bright flash of lightning appeared, followed immediately by an enormous clap of thunder that shook the house. Matthew and Christina took off screaming into the house. Brave as I am, I have never gone up a flight of stairs so fast in my life. I found Matthew and Christina huddled and screaming behind the back of the family room sofa. (The back of the sofa and the radiator for our steam heat made a little nook. Matthew and Christina used it as their clubhouse and obviously considered it the "safe zone.")

To my dismay, the children had run screaming through the house wearing sneakers covered in mud. It would have been one thing if they had been walking and left little tiny footprints. But they had been running, pounding each mud-encased sneaker into the floor with a force that only terrified children can create, splattering mud in every direction. One of them must have fallen down rounding the corner from the kitchen into the family room, as evidenced by the gigantic skid mark and the clump of mud on the baseboard. Another set of skid marks led the way into the nook behind the sofa, where the two had basically slid like baseball players stealing second base.

I put Jessica into her portable crib and went to the mouth of the "clubhouse" to survey the damage. Matthew and Christina were sitting there with their arms wrapped tightly around each other, eyes wide as saucers. It probably wasn't nice of me, but the scene was so funny that I couldn't help laughing. "You guys, that was only a thunder boomer. You two took off like your heads were on fire." I giggled.

Since I didn't seem to be afraid, Matthew became the brave big brother again. "Yeah, Steenie, you ran like your head was on fire." Matthew came out of the clubhouse and Christina jumped up and said, "My head fire" as she hit herself on the head trying to put out the imaginary fire. This cracked us all up—except for Jessica, who was sound asleep at this point.

Standing in the middle of my mud-encrusted family room, I told Matthew and Christina to give me their muddy clothes. I helped them get the muddy shoes and socks off and they finished getting the rest of their clothes off, down to Matt's Scoobys and Christina's diaper. Looking at the state of the hardwood floors in my kitchen and family room, I decided the only reasonable course of action was a good mopping. I got the mop water ready and dunked the mop head.

"You guys get a toy and sit up on the sofa while I clean the floor," I said as I started swiping at the mud in the clubhouse nook with my Mr. Clean lemon-scented mop. The kids ran to the toy box and each got a toy. Matthew came back with a plastic pirate sword and Christina ran back with a dolly dangling from its hair. "I want you two to stay on the sofa until I tell you to get down, okay?" I said as I went into the kitchen to rinse the filthy mop and reload for the next section of floor.

"Why do we have to stay on the sofa?" asked Matthew in his *this is the beginning of an argument* tone of voice.

"Because this is a magic mop," I said as I brandished the mop at the children. "It turns mud into sharks and they swim in the water left on the floors." Both Matthew and Christina were fascinated with this idea.

"How come the sharks don't eat you?" Matthew, the stickler for details, asked.

"Because I'm standing on the dry spots," I said as I followed the trail of mud out to the mud room. As I continued the clean-up, Matthew and Christina made the story of the sharks in the floor more and more elaborate.

"I see shark," Christina squealed as she pointed excitedly over the back of the sofa.

"Don't worry Steenie, if they try to come up here I'll whack off their heads with my sword," Matthew told Christina with a gallant brandishing of his pirate sword.

"They gonna get my dolly," Christina said, hugging her doll close to her chest.

"Don't worry Steenie, I'll protect you," Matthew assured her, and patted Christina on the head like a dog.

While this was going on, I cleaned the trail of mud and went back over the floor with a clean bucket of Mr. Clean. I was just about finished when the kids started to wail, "Mommy get out of the water! The sharks will get you!" Sure enough, when I looked down, I saw that I was standing on the wet hardwood floor about three feet from the sofa. "Watch out! I'm gonna have to jump for it," I said as I launched myself off the floor and smack into the middle of the sofa. The kids, a little shocked at their mom diving into the sofa like that, giggled and flopped down on top of me. "I thought you were a goner," Matthew said, and then erupted into another gale of giggles.

"What a nice ship you have," I said to the kids when their giggling had died down.

"Yes, this is our pirate ship," Matthew informed me in a serious tone of voice. "I am the captain, 'cause I have the sword." Matthew swished his sword through the air, imitating the swashbucklers he had seen on TV.

"What I be?" Christina asked as she jumped up and down on her end of the sofa. Christina always seemed to bounce when she got excited.

"You can be the mate," Matthew said authoritatively.

"What mate?" Christina asked, still bouncing at the end of the sofa.

"Not the captain," Matthew said firmly. Having heard similar conversations between these two start this way and end in a four-year-old–two-year-old verbal slugfest, I decided it was time for me to step in. "Okay, then I will be the crew." This seemed to distract them both.

"Captain Matthew, you need to set a course to that far away island over there." I pointed to the middle of the family room wall but pretended I was using a telescope to see far off on the horizon.

"Raise the anchor," Captain Matthew ordered, and Christina and I pretended to pull the anchor up from the back of the sofa. "Raise the sails," Matthew commanded, and Christina and I pretended to pull the sails up a pretend rope in the middle of the sofa. And so we were off to the far island where the sharks couldn't get us. When the thunder roared outside, we pretended the ship was caught in a storm way out at sea. We flopped about the pirate sofa as if the waves were crashing all around us, and Christina had to be saved from falling overboard by her brave brother, Captain Matthew, at least twice.

During our travels, the telephone began to ring. "Mommy, get the phone," Matthew said as if I couldn't hear it ringing.

"I'm not getting eaten up by mommy-eating sharks just to answer the phone," I insisted. "They can just call back." This sent the kids into more gales of laughter. There was no such thing as mommy-eating sharks, my two little pirates informed me.

We spent the morning sailing across the family room to far and exotic places. We were attacked by other pirates on sev-eral occasions and had to fight for our safe passage. Eventually,

Captain Matthew and his crew became hungry. Matthew checked the "water" to see if the pirate sofa had finally outrun the sharks. "Nope, the sharks are still all in these waters," Matthew explained to his mate, Christina, and his crew, mommy.

"I know," I said as I tossed my cushion from the sofa onto the floor. "We can use these as our dinghies and paddle our way to the kitchen table."

Matthew flew into a fit of laughter, "Dingy, that's what Justin calls his fire hose."

"Oh, my. Not that kind of dingy, I mean like small boats," I said as I laughed along with Matthew. Christina joined in too, but I don't think she really got the joke.

We threw the cushions on the floor and everybody dived off the sofa, then flopped around on the shark-infested hardwood floors trying to climb onto their "little boats." We paddled into the kitchen and Matthew showed us all how to use our pretend ropes to tie our boats to the legs of the kitchen chairs. We sat at the kitchen table and ate our peanut butter and jelly sandwiches and told each other about great journeys taken, battles won, and gold and treasure buried deep inside big, dark caves at the edge of the ocean.

How Much Can You Stuff Into a Minivan?

By Pam

When Jack was about six months old and Gracie was two years old, we decided to take our first family trip. My sister lived in Atlanta and hadn't met Jack yet. Scott and I figured it would be nice to make the four-hour ride to her house and spend Thanksgiving there. Okay, the truth is, we were clueless. We were novices and didn't realize all that would be involved in a four-hour car trip with two young kids, heading for a home without children—a home where there have never been children—and where the occupant (my beloved sister) had a passion for breakable antiques and non-kid-friendly furniture. Oh, and did I happen to mention two large, lovable, but definitely untrained dogs lived there as well? The top two things on my packing list were baby wipes to contend with the almost certain dog slobber fest and lots of money to pay for whatever got broken.

Being the overly worried, must-be-prepared-for-any-emergency mother that I am, I spent the morning before the trip making a list of everything that had to come with us. Now, I realize that if Kae had been in charge, packing would have been a heck of a lot easier: diapers, some clothes, a few toys, and some snacks. But it's me we're talking about here, the mother who worries that we could get stuck for days on I-75 in a blizzard—in *Georgia.* So lists were made and emergency supplies were bought. If we were to be stuck on I-75 in one of those freak, 300-year-blizzards, I would be the mommy-on-the-spot for any driver in need of batteries, flashlights, blankets, food, water, toys, diapers, or even just a stick of gum.

The packing procedure began the night before, with Scott doing the typical manly ritual of checking the car's tires and oil, cleaning the windows inside and out, and driving to the gas station to fill up the tank so we'd be set to go in the morning without delay. The manly ritual also included mapping our route. This was before we got our portable GPS, and even though I could've downloaded the route from the Internet, Scott needed to perform the age-old ritual of sitting down at the dining room table, spreading out the map, and figuring time, distance, and gas mileage. Bennett men had done it before him, and this Bennett man was carrying on the tradition.

When the route was mapped and the car passed Scott's inspection, we started packing...and packing...and packing, until there wasn't an empty suitcase or duffle bag left in the house. I carefully calculated how many diapers I might need to use for Jack and how many pull-ups for Gracie, and then packed double the amount. Stacks of wipes, suitcases filled with enough kids' clothes to last two weeks (we were going for a long weekend), and every other accessory that might come in handy were stuffed into the minivan. Looking back and being the wise old mom I am now, I realize I could've traveled a heck of a lot lighter because *they have stores in Atlanta*. If I needed them, I could have bought extra diapers. But at the time, I didn't want to take any chances that a store might not have the brand of diaper my precious little Jack's butt was used to. I also knew in the back of my nervous mommy brain that my sister did, in fact, have a washer and dryer. In case of spills, clothes could have been cleaned, but I was compelled with the need to overpack; half the clothes in the kids' closets were coming with us.

On one of my endless trips in and out of the house with an armful of miscellaneous stuff to be packed, I looked over at our DVD collection and tossed 10 or 15 DVDs for the kids to watch in the car on top of my pile. During this four-hour trip, I was going to be prepared with food, drinks, entertainment, perfect climate control, and the ability to sanitize anything and everything.

A portable crib was also going to make the trip with us for Jack to sleep in. We planned to have Gracie either sleep with us or we'd make a cozy sleeping pad for her next to our bed. In anticipation of the latter, I jammed her favorite blankets and pillow into the minivan.

My clothes and necessities were definitely an afterthought and were hastily tossed into the last available suitcase, along with Scott's few items (men really think it's okay to wear the same pants day after day after day). The difference between packing for a trip as a woman without children and packing as a mother of two was amazing. I used to make sure I had travel-size bottles of all my favorite cosmetics and toiletries, but I now was only concerned with making sure I remembered my toothbrush and floss.

The next morning, the second stage of packing began—food and perishable items. Formula, bottles, sippy cups, juice, and snacks were stowed away in coolers and bags and then shoved into the tiny bit of free space in the minivan.

After a last check of the house to make sure I didn't forget to bring a cherished toy, we rounded up the children and secured them in their car seats. We were off. Actually, we were headed two miles down the road to my mother's apartment to pick her up. She was coming with us.

My mother appeared at the door of her apartment and waved for Scott to come in. We figured she would have at least one suitcase and maybe an additional overnight case, so we made sure to leave just barely enough space in the back of the minivan. Scott got out of the van and disappeared into mom's apartment to retrieve her suitcase. While he was gone, I got out of the passenger seat and headed around to the back of the van so I could climb up into the very back fold-down seat, leaving the front passenger seat for my mother. But there was no way for me to get in. I'd have to wait for Scott to make a path for me by moving some of the items that were packed to the ceiling.

I saw Scott and my mother emerge from her apartment. Their arms were loaded with bags and boxes. This wasn't in the plan.

"What in the heck are you bringing?" I asked as they came around to the back of the van.

Scott rolled his eyes. "Your mom did some baking," he said.

"Be careful with that," my mother scolded Scott as he tried to find a spot for one of the bags. "Those cookies are fragile."

During the previous week, in anticipation of the trip, my mother baked cookies, cookies, and more cookies. She also made a cheese-cake (that had to be kept on ice) and two apple pies. These items had to be placed carefully in the car so they wouldn't be crushed and the apple pies wouldn't tip. She also packed a much larger suitcase than I expected. Apparently, my 80-year-old mother had a greater sense of fashion than I realized.

"Oh, wait," my mother said just before getting into the car, "I forgot my robe." With that, she went back into her apartment. Seconds later she reappeared with the fluffiest, bulkiest, largest terry cloth bathrobe I'd ever seen.

"Mom, we're going to Atlanta, not Alaska," I lightheartedly called out from the back of the van.

"I get cold," she replied, and handed the robe to Scott so he could perform the magical mystical feat of fitting eight pounds of terry cloth into a one-inch space in the minivan.

Scott unloaded several items from the van so I could climb into the fold-down seat. I ended up with my knees tucked tightly under my chin. Scott started shoving everything back into the van. I imag-ined the leg cramps I would be enduring within the first half-hour of the drive.

As I watched suitcases being piled to the van's ceiling and my ability to move becoming more restricted, I tried to look on the bright side of being a human sardine for the next four hours: I would be able to watch the movie on the DVD player with the kids while

Scott got stuck in conversation with my mother. Luckily, I had pre-loaded the DVD player with a kiddie movie that I would be able to somewhat enjoy, instead of having to endure two hours of *Winnie the Pooh* or *Blue's Clues.*

To this day, I am still in awe of Scott's ability to use every square inch of a minivan to accommodate three adults, two children, six weeks' worth of luggage, half a toy store, the portable crib from hell, coolers, a cheesecake, two apple pies, and a potty seat. He did it, and although once in the car I wouldn't be able to get out until we reached our final destination, and the cheesecake had to rest atop the potty seat, we were loaded and ready for our first family trip!

As is typically the case when you plan everything perfectly, nature does its own thing. Halfway through the trip Jack pooped in his diaper—and I mean he *pooped*. He managed to time it for seconds after we passed an exit, so we all had to endure the toxic fumes for several miles until Scott could find a safe place to pull off the interstate. My fold-down seat was immediately behind Jack. I was dead center in the middle of something quite incompatible: the aroma of apple pie and baby poop.

Scott was a trouper and took care of Jack's diaper. He also took care of Gracie's frequent need for potty breaks as well as his own need to stretch his legs and make a bathroom pit stop. Me? I was trapped, and tested my bladder's elasticity to its limit. So while Scott and my mother sipped soda, munched on cookies, and chatted away in the front seat, I tried not to think about my dry throat and need to pee. Instead, I started calculating in my mind how much money I'd have to save for us to afford an RV.

Cookies for Dinner

By Kae

When Matthew began eating baby food, I invented games like the airplane, flying tiny spoonfuls of pureed nutrition into his mouth as if it was a hangar. If the airplane didn't work, we shifted to the choo

choo—tiny spoonfuls chugged their way toward Matthew's open mouth, ending in my best imitation of a train horn as he clamped his lips down on the spoon. If the pureed nutrition was something that was not to Matthew's liking, he blew it out of his mouth like a whale surfacing for air. I spent many a morning scraping dried pureed rejects from my kitchen floor.

Matthew was generally a hearty eater. He was very thin and tall for his age. When he began eating solid foods, I rushed to my *All the Goofy Advice About Babydom* reference shelf for guidance. I introduced all the right foods in the right order. If Matthew showed a dislike for a certain food, I replaced it at that meal with something I knew he did like. It was always more important to me that he ate his dinner, not what the dinner consisted of. Feeding time at the Allen zoo was peaceful. Until Matthew learned to talk.

Matthew progressed from baby food to real people food without a blip. During this stage, most evenings Matthew and I ate dinner alone, while a plate of congealing food sat in the oven waiting for David to come home from work.

As Matthew turned from two to three, though, he entered the picky eater stage pretty much overnight. This is when I learned a powerful lesson: It wasn't about the food; it was his perception of the food that determined whether he would eat it.

Every night when I started dinner, Matthew sat at the kitchen table and colored in his coloring book. Since I had heard numerous horror stories from the other mothers at Matthew's preschool about their children drawing on their walls with crayons, I didn't have crayons lying all around the house. The crayons were kept on top of the refrigerator. They only came out when I was in the kitchen cooking. This set-up solved two important issues for me. One was how to keep Matthew occupied in the kitchen while I pre-pared dinner and the other was how to keep graffiti off my living room walls.

"Mommy, what's for dinner?" Matthew asked every night when I started dinner.

"Spaghetti," I said this night as I put the water on to boil.

"I don't like besketti," Matthew informed me with his very serious face.

"Well, Matthew, you love spaghetti. We had it just last week and you loved it."

"I don't like besketti today." And he refused to eat it.

At first I struggled with this newfound power my son had—the power to say no at the dinner table. I followed in the footsteps of my parents and probably their parents: You stay at the table until you have eaten your dinner. Of course, this never worked on me when I was a kid, and my little nut didn't fall far from the tree. Matthew was just stubborn enough to sit there, and sit there, and sit there, until finally it was time for bath and bed.

After several nights of his refusing to eat and several nights of sitting and waiting and putting Matthew to bed hungry, something had to change. The next evening Matthew had his bath before dinner because we had played outside all day and he was filthy. I brought Matthew, freshly scrubbed, into the kitchen and started making dinner.

"What's for dinner, mommy?" Matthew asked while working hard to color a dinosaur with a green crayon.

"Tonight we are having cookies for dinner," I said to Matthew in my happiest voice.

"Cookies!" Matthew was elated. Finally, he had worn me down and we were having something great to eat.

"Yep, we are having these really yummy cookies mommy just found the recipe for."

When the "cookies" were ready, I spooned them into his Batman bowl and handed him a spoon. He dug in and had eaten all the way to where Batman was peeking up from the bottom of the bowl when the telephone rang.

"Matthew, daddy's on the phone for you."

"Daddy, we're having cookies for dinner!" Matthew said excitedly.

I spent the next few minutes calming David down on the phone. No, I was not feeding Matthew cookies. It was actually chicken and dumplings, but I told Matthew they were cookies and he had eaten more at this meal than he had the entire week before.

For the longest time, dinnertime "cookies" were synonymous for chicken and dumplings. Matthew finally began eating spaghetti again, too, but I told him we were having worms for dinner.

Creaky Floors

By Pam

After bringing my four-month-old daughter home, I joined the club of the sleep-deprived mothers—those walking zombies who have no memory of dressing in the morning and no energy to comb their own hair, and who occasionally put the dirty socks in the dishwasher. (Oh come now, don't tell me you've never confused the dishwasher with the washing machine!)

There would be no more uninterrupted nights for me. My middle-aged body that had gotten quite used to being able to dictate just how much shut-eye it needed was no longer in charge. A cute little diaper-clad alarm clock was now the dictator.

At seven in the evening, I would begin the ritual of attempting to get my daughter to sleep. I did all the things millions of mothers have done before me: give the baby a warm bath, then get her dried, powdered, diapered, and rewarded with a warm bottle. This was my absolute favorite time with Gracie. I sat in the chair with my new daughter cradled in my arms as she had her bottle. My husband read a bedtime story and then I lovingly carried Gracie to her crib. As much as I cherished that tender, quiet moment before bedtime, I knew it was always the start of the nightly ritual of trying everything I could think of to get Gracie to simply close her eyes and go to sleep.

Being the over-informed mother, I purchased all the gadgets and gizmos the experts said would send my child off to dreamland. Yes, I'm a sucker for a gadget—as Kae would probably be the first to tell you. I had the soft, soothing four-watt nightlight (seven-watt was too bright), the ultimate battery-operated mobile, the latest and greatest sound-and-lights aquarium, and the sound machine that made a soft whooshing noise to comfort my baby. I then stood over the crib with Gracie in my arms, softly singing a lullaby to her. Her eyes would start to close and I'd very gently place her in her crib.

In other households this might have been the perfect ending, but not in mine.

As soon as Gracie realized she was in a crib and no longer in my arms, she wailed. Some of the books I read said to pick up the baby and soothe her, while others said to let her cry it out. Since we were still trying to bond and I knew my little daughter had just experienced major separation trauma, I didn't feel that letting her cry it out was the thing to do. So I picked her up. She snuggled into me, and I was one happy mommy...momentarily. When she was just about in dreamland again, I placed her back in the crib. The instant her diapered bottom made contact with mattress, it sent a message to her brain to instruct her lungs to hit the panic button. Perhaps this was how opera singer Beverly Sills started out. To this day, I'm surprised the mirror over the dresser didn't shatter.

One night, while in the middle of the nightly ritual, I made a discovery. As long as I kept my hand on Gracie when I placed her in the crib, she remained calm. *Okay, I can do that,* I thought. *I'll just stand over the crib and gently stroke her hair until she goes to sleep. Yippee, hallelujah, she finally drifted off.* I slowly and carefully stepped away from the crib, thinking I had finally found the way to ease her to sleep. I tiptoed backward, inching out of the room, when it became horribly apparent that we had creaky floors and Gracie had amazing hearing. Our floor was covered in carpet but even that didn't sufficiently muffle the sound. Squeak, groan, creak—Gracie heard it and her eyes popped open and the wailing started.

Back to her crib I went to resume the hair stroking ritual. When she was asleep I again attempted to walk out of the room, taking giant steps to avoid what I thought were the squeaky areas. But there were no quiet areas. Squeak, groan, creak—here were go again. How could I be married to a carpenter and have creaky floors?

Thinking that if I distributed my weight more evenly, the squeaking wouldn't be so loud, I got down on my hands and knees and tried to crawl out of the room. I made it all the way to the bedroom door, but when I stood up, I hit the squeakiest, creakiest part of the floor. Gracie woke up, we did the hair stroking routine again, and then I crawled out, being careful to crawl all the way into the hallway.

The stroking-crawling routine became the norm at bedtime. It got to where I could accurately identify exactly what route to take out of the bedroom. Of course, it wasn't a straight route. I had to navigate around the edge of the room to avoid the squeakiest floor boards. Why didn't I just have Scott fix the floor, you might be asking. He did make several trips under the house, but even his formidable skills were no match for our singing floor boards.

Every time Gracie woke up during the night, I stroked and crawled. Scott offered to help when Gracie awoke late at night, but he didn't know the bedroom terrain the way I did. He had the stroking part down but couldn't outsmart the floor boards. Only mommy knew the secret path.

The Shopping Show

By Kae

When you have children in tow, any errand, no matter how small, can become an adventure. I still maintain that the best time to run errands with children is just after breakfast or just after they get a nap and a snack. By the time I had my third child, grocery shopping had been relegated to the morning slot. The real reason for this is that grocery shopping with all three kids was such an ordeal that I would put it off as long as absolutely possible. The day I realized that lunch was going to be the dregs in the peanut butter jar, slathered on pudgy little fingers, it was grocery shopping day.

The first step in going on any errand was gathering the troops. First, everyone in the house had to make the potty run. Luckily for me, Matthew took his role as Christina's potty mentor seriously and was more than happy to take the lead in the "tell me questions" game while I changed Jessica's diaper. Next, the diaper bag had to be loaded with all the things necessary for any trip outside the house: diapers for the baby, a change of clothes for each of the kids, a box of large diaper wipes, two Ziploc bags of Cheerios, two small sippy cups, and one bottle of mother's milk for Jessica. While I put Jessica into her infant carrier, Matthew put on his shoes and Christina tried to put on hers.

Every time we tied the kids' shoes, no matter what else was going on, we had to tell the bunny story. I had taught Matthew to tie his shoes by telling him a story based on how you manipulate the laces. To start, one lace went under the other one and I said, "The first bunny rabbit ran down in the hole." Next we made a loop in one of the strings. "The rabbit's hole was under a big tree." Then we wrapped the other lace around the "tree" and poked part of it through the hole that was created. "Then the second bunny rabbit ran around the tree and right down the hole." Finally, we pulled the two loops until the knot was tight. "Then the doggie came and pulled the bunny's ears tight." Matthew always giggled his head off when the doggie pulled the bunny's ears.

Once everyone had gone to the potty, shoes were on the right feet and tied tight, the purse and diaper bag were slung over my right shoulder, and the baby was in her car carrier perched on my jutted-out left hip, we headed out the back door.

With all three kids strapped into their car seats, we made the short trip down the road to the grocery store. The shopping adventure really began in the parking lot. First I had to find a place to park that was fairly close to the store. When you have a newborn and a two-year-old, you have to be aware of where you leave your car. If you make the mistake of parking too far away from the store, you will end up in the middle of a busy parking lot with a child-turned-mule, trying to drag her toward the automatic front doors. It was not uncommon for the cashiers in the store to see me trudging across the parking lot with the infant car carrier perched on one hip, purse and diaper bag over my shoulder, Christina wrapped around my neck like a monkey, and Matthew holding onto my purse strap.

Inside the store, I put Matthew and Christina in the deep part of one cart and put Jessica in her car seat in the front basket. Then I got another cart to put the food in. The train system of shopping developed out of necessity. Where else could I put the kids where they would not wander away or grab everything on the shelves?

When I had just Matthew, he would sit it the front basket of the cart and hold the shopping list. Yes, at one time I actually wrote down all the necessary purchases, planned out meals and lunches in advance, and knew exactly how many Cokes and bottles of juice I needed to buy to make it to the next shopping trip. I would meticulously record these needs on a long white piece of paper, usually in the order in which they could be found in the grocery store aisles. Unfortunately, by the time my third child arrived, the meticulously planned shopping excursions ended. By the time I got the kids and all their gear into the car then out of the car at the store, made the trek across the parking lot, pulled out the carts and settled the kids into their cart, I would dig furiously in my purse only to realize that the meticulously prepared list was still sitting on the kitchen counter. My solution was to ditch the list and just wander up and down the aisles. Yes, we sometimes ended up with three bottles of dishwasher soap and no aluminum foil, but we almost always had toilet paper and cereal.

So up and down each aisle we would go, a small blonde woman pushing one cart in front of her with her right hand while she pulled a second cart behind her with her left hand—all the while keeping up an incessant chatter with the kids about what kind of fruit to buy, whether they liked potatoes, holding their noses as we passed the fish counter, and distracting them when we passed the ice cream section.

Some of the other shoppers found our little dog and pony show amusing, others glared. It was always the young single people who glared. They had no idea what it was like to attempt to entertain two toddlers and keep an infant fat and happy while procuring the week's nutritional needs. So they were not amused as I handed Matthew a can of green beans so that he could "scan" them into the cart, making sure that Christina made an appropriate "beep" noise indicating that the scanned item had been recorded. Every once in awhile when I had PMS or was otherwise feeling hateful, I would follow some glaring adolescent down each aisle just to give them a glimpse of what their lives would be like in the next five or so years.

Frankly, I think there is no better birth control for a 19-year-old girl than to be stalked by a babbling woman, three kids, and two grocery carts up and down the 18 aisles of the Piggly Wiggly.

As if the dragging and babbling and shopping and stalking weren't difficult enough, the final stage of the shopping experience was akin to trial by fire. Whoever had the grand idea to put the candy right next to where you wait to check out was the devil himself for all the mothers who have to grocery shop with their young children. Cashiers would cringe when they saw me coming with my cart full of little time bombs, dragging an overloaded cart of nutritional needs.

Early in our shopping experiences, I had an epiphany: If the kids don't anticipate that they will get candy from the checkout aisle, they will be less likely to start the begging-whining form of parental persuasion. Being me, I had to take this idea one step further. It was made very clear to my kids that if they even *asked* if they could have something from the candy shelves the answer would be no—not just for that trip, but for several trips thereafter. My reward was a stress-free exit from the grocery store.

My other reward was seeing the truly amazed look on the kids' faces when every once in a blue moon they were allowed to pick out a piece of candy to have after their naps.

Chapter 9

What's a Crisis?

Jack-in-the-Box

By Pam

When Scott and I adopted Gracie, we lived in a four-bedroom house. Since my husband and I each had our own business, we had converted two of the bedrooms into offices. That left us with one master bedroom and one bedroom for Gracie. At the time, we weren't planning on adopting another child. Less than a year later, however, we changed our minds.

As we sent off all our adoption paperwork and began the emotional and unbearable process of waiting to hear if there would be an answer to our prayers, we looked around our house and realized we didn't have enough room. The two bedrooms we had converted into offices were small, so there was no way we could combine them into one big office for the two of us. We talked about moving, but we had already done so much renovation work on our home and we loved where we lived. So the logical solution was to add on. After all, Scott is in the construction business.

We decided to build a new master suite and move Gracie into the old master bedroom. Then our new son could have Gracie's current room. We had a plan—or so we thought.

Home remodeling television shows make everything look so easy but projects always take twice as long and cost twice as much as you expect. If the weather doesn't cause major delays, then workers who don't show up or back-ordered material will. We were no exception. My husband being in the construction business didn't really help. When a big construction job came along, Scott had to pull his crew off our project. Do you know the old saying about the cobbler's kids going barefoot? That was us.

The delay wouldn't have been so bad, but as luck would have it, we received that much-anticipated phone call announcing that our son in Guatemala was officially ours before our remodeling job was finished.

Okay don't panic, I told myself. *I'm already a mother so I'm used to crises. I can figure this out.* I decided we could just put our son's crib in our bedroom or in Gracie's room. It would all work out.

What we found out, though, was that our new son, Jack, was the lightest sleeper on the planet. If my husband or I tried to roll over in bed and the mattress springs squeaked just a little, Jack would hear it and wake up crying. Gracie was a restless sleeper who would often jabber to herself during the night, so there was no way Jack's crib could go in that room, either. He needed a room of his own or no one was going to get any sleep. But where?

With the ongoing renovation, Scott had temporarily lost his office because that was the wall where the construction started. My office was now piled high with Scott's stuff until the work was finished. Our choices were few. We knew we needed Jack to be close by, but not so close that we'd disturb his sleep. An unusual but possible solution appeared before me as I was getting dressed one morning: *the master closet.* Okay, I know what you're thinking, but it's a relatively large closet and it even has a window. If I removed the clothes, it would be comparable to a very, very small nursery.

We were desperate for options and this seemed to be the best choice. If Jack ended up in therapy as an adult because he slept in the closet for a month as a four-and-a-half-month-old baby, then so be it. I figured there would be plenty of things I'd do as mother that might mean my kids ended up on a therapist's couch, so if this was going to be the first of many reasons, I'd just have to live with it. In addition to their college funds, I'd start a therapy fund.

Even though the closet was a good size, it wasn't large enough to set up a traditional crib. It would, however, handle a portable crib, and we just happened to have one leftover from when Gracie was a baby. I set the crib up, installed a mobile on one end, and lovingly placed a few stuffed animals on my clothing shelves to make the closet less of a...well...less of a closet. A Winnie the Pooh nightlight finished off the decor, and the place was ready for Jack.

This was not the way I wanted to start our life with my new son, but with luck, construction would be finished in a month. After a few days, it started to seem normal to have a crib in my closet and teddy bears sitting atop the sweaters on my shelves. I didn't even mind that Gracie referred to her new baby brother as "Jack-in-the-box" because of the size of his accommodations.

A few days after we came home with Jack, the social worker in charge of his adoption called. In addition to the initial home study evaluation, the social worker must make a few visits to the house after the child is home. She was calling to schedule the first post-placement appointment. This sent me into a panic. What would she think of me putting Jack in the closet? Would this be grounds for losing my child? Would she understand that he would soon have a very nice room of his own? Sure she would. Who wouldn't understand construction delays? Would Gracie announce to her that we kept Jack in a box? I wasn't going to take any chances.

On the morning of the appointment, I cleaned the house from top to bottom. If you know anyone who has adopted a child, you probably know that their home will never look as spotless as it does during the adoption process. Those of us who want to be adoptive parents know that we have good character, high morals, and will give the child a wonderful life, but we panic that we'll be rejected by the adoption agency if guests can't lick the floors. So I over-cleaned, over-dressed, and over-worried. And my house was sparkling. Every pet hair and microscopic food crumb were eradicated from each carpet fiber.

Next on my list was to move Jack's crib into the master bedroom. In hindsight, I know it would have been perfectly acceptable to leave the crib in the closet and explain the situation, but those first few days after adoption a new mother is so filled with panic that the baby will be taken away if you so much as put him in the wrong diaper or have his hair parted on the wrong side. Of course, it's not really like that, but new mother emotions can really cloud a normally sensible woman's judgment.

With my kids happily playing in the master bedroom, I attempted to move the portable crib. The door to the closet was much too narrow, so the crib would have to be dismantled. My mind wandered back to the night I assembled the crib. It seemed relatively easy—after all, it's a crib designed for travel so it's made for quick assembly, right? Well, the assembling part may have been easy but the dismantling process wasn't going well. It didn't matter how much tugging, pushing, pulling, grunting, pleading, begging, and crying I did, this crib was not coming apart. I could only get it to fold up halfway.

I looked at my watch and the social worker was due to arrive in 25 minutes. Stepping into the bathroom, I looked at my reflection in the mirror. My Relaxed and Experienced Mother appearance was gone, replaced by my Please Don't Take My Baby Away appearance. No time to worry now about how I looked. I had to get that crib out of the closet. I ran into my office and got a measuring tape. I measured the width of the closet door and the current width of the partially folded crib. If I didn't mind that there might be some loss of paint on the door, I could probably squeeze the crib through the opening.

Gracie, curious about all the grunting noises coming from her mother, came to see what I was doing. "Mommy, why are you taking Jack's crib out of the box?"

"It's not a box, honey," I corrected her while wiping sweat from my face. "It's a closet—a very big closet."

"Isn't Jack going to live in the box anymore?" she asked.

"He doesn't live in a *box*, Gracie," I insisted, "he just sleeps in this part of the house while we're making the house bigger."

Gracie looked at me and then at the crib. I knew that in her mind, Jack lived in a box and that was that. I was wondering if I could convince Gracie to take a very early nap so she'd be asleep when the social worker arrived. Either that or I'd give her a snack that would make it difficult for her to talk—maybe a peanut butter sandwich or dry saltines. No time to think about that now, though; the portable crib was stuck halfway out of the closet.

After much struggling and losing a little skin off the knuckles of both of my hands, I still couldn't wrangle that crib out of the closet. *Oh, the heck with it,* I thought. *I'll just have to explain to the social worker that this was the best option for the crib.* I convinced myself that I was being foolish in thinking Jack could be taken away from me because of where we kept his crib. So I started tugging on the portable crib to get it back to its original position in the closet. It wouldn't budge. The partially folded crib was stuck in the closet doorway. I pulled and yanked but it wasn't going anywhere.

Okay, don't panic, Pam. I'll just call Scott and have him come home and help me. I looked at my watch and realized the social worker was due in 15 minutes. There was no time for Scott to get home. The crib would just have to stay wedged in the doorway. My next problem was that I was standing in the closet and the crib was blocking my exit. I heard a car door slam. I looked out the closet window and saw the social worker getting out of her car. She was early, the crib was wedged in the doorway, and I was stuck in the closet. *Perfect!*

Panic can create such athletic strength in a normally out-of-shape, non-athletic woman. As the social worker was climbing the stairs onto my front porch, I tried to hoist myself up and over the stuck crib. I might have made it on the first attempt, but my jeans were a bit too tight. When I got dressed that day I hadn't antici-pated that I'd have to climb out of my closet. So I stripped off my jeans, tossed them over, and then climbed up and over the crib. Once safely on the other side, I pulled my jeans back on, raced to the bathroom sink, splashed my face with cold water, and ran Gracie's Cinderella comb through my hair.

Gracie stared at me with an open mouth. I patted her on the head. "Hopefully, you won't remember any of this when you grow up," I said.

As the doorbell rang, I scooped Jack up, perched him on my hip, and walked down the hallway toward the front door. Gracie skipped along beside me, holding my hand. I was the picture of motherhood.

My visit with the social worker went smoothly. We sat in the living room while the kids played. I smiled and chatted happily, and one would never know that there was a mangled portable crib suspended in a doorway on the other side of my house. The social worker asked me several questions about how Jack was adjusting and said it was obvious that he seemed to be a happy, content little baby. She never asked to see his room or any other areas of the house. I had been prepared to confess all my foolishness, but breathed quite a huge sigh of relief when the social worker stood up to leave. Things were going to be okay after all. My little secret would stay a secret and I wouldn't lose Jack just because I was keeping him in a closet.

"Bye, Jack," the social worker said as she approached the front door. "You look sleepy. I'll bet it's time for your nap."

Just then, a big truck rumbled by on the street, making lots of noise.

"He's Jack-in-the-box," Gracie's voice came from behind me. "He sleeps in a box. Mommy tried to take his crib out of the box but it won't come out. It's stuck in the door. Mommy took off her pants and jumped over his crib and I saw her underwear."

I held my breath and smiled innocently at the social worker.

"Gracie, did you say something? I couldn't hear you because of the truck," replied the social worker as she stood at the open doorway.

Gracie paused, shrugged her shoulders, and said, "Bye-bye."

"Bye-bye," said the social worker. I closed and locked the door behind her.

I looked at Gracie, who was giving me a huge smile. "Cookie please, mommy?" she sweetly asked.

As a pay-off, a cookie was a bargain.

The Bird

By Kae

By the time Jessica was 18 months old, I had been changing diapers for seven and a half years straight. By this time I estimate that I had changed approximately 20,000 diapers. Needless to say, this activity had become second nature. Out of those 20,000 diaper changes, there were only a few that stood out as significant.

This day, Jessica's morning boom-boom had arrived and it was time for diaper change 20,001. I scooped her up from the floor and carried her off to the changing table in her bedroom. Jessica's nursery was a small sun room off the back of our house. Actually, it was originally a small kitchen that was added to the house in 1920 when the then-owner converted the house into two apartments. This little 1920s kitchen was the perfect size for a nursery. There was just enough room for a crib, a dresser, and a changing table.

Laying Jessica down on the changing table, I pulled her arms above her head and kissed her little face and neck. Making loud kissing sounds next to her ear was always rewarded with gales of giggles.

"You are mommy's favorite brown-eyed girl," I sing-songed to her while assembling the requisite diaper change paraphernalia. It was okay if she was my favorite brown-eyed girl; Christina had blue eyes and was my favorite blue-eyed girl. Matthew got to be my favorite boy.

With a flourish, I grabbed the snaps on her pants and with a great big *ta dah!* I pulled the fabric so all the snaps would come undone. Jessica giggled and kicked her feet. Then I pulled the unsnapped legs of the pants up around her waist so I could assess the damage without having to do an entire wardrobe change.

I never had any patience when it came to diaper changing. I have watched other mothers struggle to get a child to lie still while changing a diaper. I have actually witnessed a mother attempting to change a child's diaper while the child was standing up and walking away. The last thing I wanted to do was attempt to get a poop-filled diaper off a child's butt while chasing him or her around the house. So from birth it was an unwritten rule in our house: If your pants are full of poop, you need to lie down and be still until mom says it's okay to move. I'm sure each one of the kids made the error of not being still during a diaper change. This is when they found out the importance of having more than thin air between their bottom and the palm of my hand.

Pulling back the tabs on Jessica's diaper, I opened the front and peered in to assess the damage. Quickly, I slammed the diaper shut. "Jessica Paige, what have you done in there?" I opened the diaper again and peered in. Then I slammed the diaper shut again, "Jessica Paige, I think something died in your diaper, little missy," I said as I tickled her under the ribcage on both sides.

"No died—poo poo."

"I don't know, this is so stinky..." Once again an image of canary yellow rubber gloves—the kind my grandmother used to wear—floated through my mind. But alas, I still had never purchased yellow rubber gloves and had to go in armed with nothing more than a diaper wipe—generic at that. With a deftness that only 20,000 diaper changes can account for, I wiped, swiped, powdered, and freshly diapered my child's behind. I pulled the pants down from her waist and snapped the two sides of the legs together.

Now, no diaper change is complete without a round of tickles and giggles and numerous loud *zerberts* on the tender tummy. Once the tickles, zerberts, and giggles were accomplished, I turned my attention to the dirty diaper. I put the wipes inside and then rolled it up in a nice little package and sealed it closed with the recloseable diaper tabs. Confident that the "package" inside was completely contained, I turned to pitch it into the garbage can that sat on the floor by the head of the changing table.

At first, I was sure I was mistaken. Maybe the fumes from the diaper were causing me to hallucinate. Then I realized, *this is real.* Sitting right on the edge of the wastebasket was the biggest, blackest crow I had ever seen in my entire life. There we stood, a woman frozen in the act of spiking a poopie diaper into the trash and a two-foot tall black crow staring her right in the face. The bird never moved. It stared me down like a gambler holding four aces. It had shiny black bead eyes and a black beak that looked long enough to dig through the hardwood floor of Edgar Allan Poe's *The Tell-Tale Heart.*

I slowly lowered the diaper onto the top of the changing table and ever so slowly scooped Jessica up in my arms. "Let's go find daddy," I whispered to Jessica as I backed up toward the nursery door. The crow followed us with his beady black eyes but never ruffled a feather. I backed out the nursery door into the hall and quietly pulled the door shut. Then I started yelling, "David, David, come quick."

There are some things you know about your husband before you get married, like he doesn't eat beans. Then there are things you learn as the circumstances arise, like he stinks at discipline. One thing I never thought would become an issue in our marriage was who was going capture the wildlife when it invaded our home. The defining line was quite clear in my mind: Men change the flat tires on the car and eradicate vermin or fowl from the old homestead. Women birth the children. Not really a fair trade-off, but if it means I don't have to chase a bird around the house hoping it won't peck my eyes out, I can live with that.

David rushed into the back hall. "What?"

"There's a big black crow the size of Jessica sitting on the diaper pail in her room."

"What?"

"There's a big black crow in Jessica's room. It was sitting on the diaper pail—just sitting there staring at us. It didn't move the whole time I was goofing around changing her diaper. If it had moved I probably would have had a heart attack."

David went into Matthew's bedroom and came out with his butterfly net. *Okay,* I thought, *if he thinks he is going to catch a bird the size of a toddler with a flipping butterfly net, more power to him.* David handed me the butterfly net. *Okay, so he is going to get some other supplies to help him remove the large black crow from Jessica's bedroom.* Then he reached out and took Jessica from my arms. It was quickly becoming apparent that David would be birthing our fourth child.

In I went, armed with nothing more than a flimsy butterfly net. David was standing in relative safety in the back hallway, holding Jessica in his arms with a large towel draped over their heads in case the bird escaped the nursery and made a beeline for their eyeballs.

The crow sat on the edge of the diaper pail and followed my movement with his eyes as I came in the room brandishing my butterfly net. I immediately started up a dialogue with the bird so that he/she would understand that I was not going to hurt him/her. "Okay, you really pretty black bird. See, I need to pop this butterfly net over your head so that I can gently scoop you up and put you outside where birds belong. I'm not going to hurt you." I said all of this to the bird but hadn't moved more than a foot inside the room. From this distance I would need an elephant net to capture the poor crow.

Slowly, I began to close the distance between myself and the crow, all the time keeping up an inane stream of babble about how cute it was and how I had no desire to hurt it and would appreciate it if it didn't fly up and peck my eyeballs out before I could "rescue" it. Since I am not a very big person and my weapon of choice was a six-year-old's butterfly net, I was going to have to get about a foot and a half away from the bird before I could even hope to pop the net over its head. I continued my slow progress forward, trying not to spook the giant bird into pecking me to death. Scenes from the movie *The Birds* kept playing over and over in my mind. If determined birds could break through the glass of a telephone booth, what use was a six-year-old's butterfly net?

Slowly, I inched my way into prime bird capture distance. I was hoping that if I went slowly enough, the bird wouldn't know what was happening and I could swoop the net down on it before it figured things out. You always hear about birds having tiny brains, but they also have really small heads, so for all I know this bird was Einstein. I didn't want to underestimate my adversary. I spoke directly to the bird using my calming voice to make sure it didn't get the impression that I was trying to capture it for food or to make a shiny black feather boa. I moved slowly and cautiously because I don't know enough about birds to know if they have a fight or flight instinct. If they do, I didn't want to trigger the fight part. Actually, I didn't want to trigger the flight part, either.

Eventually, I got within striking distance and slowly began to raise the butterfly net above my head. The bird, realizing it was in imminent danger of capture, took flight in the small room. Immediately two thoughts crossed my mind. One: Protect your eyes. Two: Birds don't have sphincter muscles and the last thing I want to do in this small space is scare the poop out of a giant crow.

In an effort to protect myself, I hit the floor and held the butterfly net above my head. Maybe if this crow went into attack mode, it would get hung up in the netting and my eyes and brain would be spared death by pecking.

The bird finally settled down on the floor next to the crib. Behind me was a towel that I had forgotten to put into the laundry after Jessica's last bath. Finally, my less-than-stellar housekeeping skills were going to pay off. I grabbed the towel and threw it across the room like a fishing net. The crow was caught off guard and the towel landed directly on top of it. Cautiously, in case the crow was lulling me into a false sense of security, I approached the towel-shrouded bird.

I quickly grabbed up the bird and the towel and clutched them to my chest. Then I rushed to the nursery door and flung it open. I was greeted in the back hallway by David and Jessica. Both were still huddled underneath the towel in case the bird got away and attempted to peck their eyes out. I turned the corner and made a beeline for the back door. Once outside, I placed the towel-ensconced bird on the grass in our backyard. I grabbed the corner of the towel and quickly released the bird, making sure to run like the dickens to the middle of the driveway in case it was pissed off at having been manhandled (womanhandled?) that way. The bird stood in the yard for a few seconds, shaking off the trauma, then spread its wings and took off for parts unknown.

I turned around and there were David and Jessica, still huddled under their towel, their eyes fixed on the bird as it flew away. Jessica was too young to understand what had just happened, but I could tell from the look on David's face that I was his hero.

Panic Vacuuming

By Pam

Before becoming a mother, I could let my immaturity and irrational fears run rampant. Now, as the mother of two young children, I had to lead by example. That's all fine and dandy if you're talking about being brave in front of the kids as you kill a tiny spider (notice I said "tiny") or sleep without a nightlight, but when you get into big issues like getting lost, running out of gas, or losing your cell phone, it takes all your courage and best acting abilities to display sensible behavior. In crisis situations, the child in you fights with Mature Mommy for control.

Severe weather is a perfect example. We live in Tennessee and the threat of tornadoes is relatively high. If there's a chance of rain, there's a chance of tornadoes—it goes with the territory. I've always taken the appropriate precautions if things start to look dicey, but until recently we had never had any really close calls.

At the time, Gracie was three and a half years old and Jack was one and a half. The weather that day was on and off rain, but the forecasters were warning that severe weather was fast approaching. Scott was on the other side of town and there were multiple tornado watches and warnings. It wasn't safe for him to leave his office and return home, so it was up to me to be Brave Mommy and prepare the house.

My children were already upset by the weather, but it had more to do with the fact that it meant they couldn't watch a DVD than with any fear for their personal safety. I was explaining why we had to turn the TV off when the first hail storm began. It was the first time my kids had seen hail and they were jumping up and down at the thought of going outside to play with the "snowballs."

"You can't go outside because it's not safe. No one goes outside during hail," I said in my most Sympathetic Mommy voice.

Gracie, ever the authority on all things fun and dangerous said, "Yes they do."

"People don't play in hail, Gracie," I corrected her while trying to pry my two children away from the windows.

"I want to go outside," she insisted.

I had no choice but to use my Big Mommy voice. "No!"

"Why?" she whined and pressed her face back to the window.

"It's not safe," I repeated while attempting once again to pull her away from the window.

"Yes it is." The whine was getting more intense and she had Jack backing her up by conveniently displaying little tears on the edges of his eyelids. "Pleeeeeeez, can we go outside?"

"No!" I was growing tired of this and had bigger things on my mind, such as worrying whether the roof was going to cave in from the hail.

"Why?" she demanded.

"Because I said so!" There, I'd said it! I put my hand to my mouth in disbelief. My own mother's voice had magically come out of my mouth—the words I swore I'd never say to my kids. I had crossed a line. I was no longer just a mother; I had become *my mother.* What would be next? Eat all your dinner because there are children starving in India? Don't crack your knuckles or they'll grow really big? Don't swallow your gum because it will stay in your stomach forever? Don't frown or your face will freeze that way?

Stop it, I said to myself. I'd have to worry about the psychological damage I'm doing to my children later. Right now I had to secure the house and create a makeshift tornado shelter. If the house was still standing tomorrow, I planned on calling Kae to ask her whether declaring, "Because I said so" meant I was on the road to becoming Mommy Dearest.

Hail can be unsettling under normal conditions, but when you have multiple skylights in the house it's downright terrifying. The near-shattering sound of those rock-hard pellets assaulting my windows jerked me back into crisis mode.

"Skylights are meant to withstand that type of weather," Scott tried to reassure me via telephone.

"What? I can't hear you." I tried to make out what he was saying, but the deafening sound of hail the size of golf balls pounding on skylight glass was making it difficult. It didn't matter what he said, anyway, because I was sure that any safety tests done on the skylights didn't include hail that was fast approaching the size of cantaloupes.

Brave Mommy was not taking any chances. It was time to prepare the tornado shelter. I had always heard that the safest place is in a room without windows. Darn my husband for listening to my requests for a house with lots of sunlight. Why did he insist on giving me the floor-to-ceiling windows and multiple skylights of my dreams? Why didn't he realize we needed one underground cement cave just for situations like this?

We only had one room without a window, and that was an extra bathroom the size of a closet. It would have to do. I tracked down my two cats, who were hiding in absolute panic under my bed. I took two cat carriers out of the closet and headed toward the bedroom.

"Are we going for a ride with the cats, mommy?" Gracie asked excitedly.

"No, dear," I said, walking down the hall with a carrier under each arm.

"What are you doing?" she asked as she followed along behind me.

I told her, "Go in your room and get a couple of your favorite dolls. Help Jack get a couple of toys as well.

"Why?" she asked with a wrinkled face.

"We're going to play a game in the bathroom," I replied.

"It's not fun in the bathroom," Gracie announced as she stopped following me and stood by the window. "I want to watch the falling snowballs."

"It'll be fun," I promised, hoping that my Kae instincts would take over and I'd come up with something entertaining other than watching the roof get ripped from the house. "Please stay away from the window."

"Why?" came the obvious question from Gracie.

And of course, since I now knew that my mother was indeed living inside of me, I had no choice but to do her proud by once again responding, "Because I said so!"

My answer stopped the kids in their tracks. They turned and headed to their rooms to get their toys. Wow, I could get used to pulling out that powerful phrase when needed. Being a mother should come with some perks that don't need justification or explanation. "Because I said so" could actually cover a lot of territory for me. Eat your vegetables because I said so. Go to bed because I said so. Sit down because I said so. Stand up because I said so. *Stop!* I could see the potential to become mad with power.

"Mommy, why are you just standing there with the cat carriers?" Gracie asked as she and Jack stood in the hallway with their chosen toys. Okay, time to get back to reality. Power-Hungry Mommy would have to wait until Brave Mommy took take care of the immediate crisis. Get the cats, grab the kids, and create a shelter. The hail was getting bigger and the sky was getting darker. No time to lose.

I headed back down the hallway with my kids trailing behind, put the cats in their carriers, and put the carriers in the shower stall of the tiny bathroom that was about to be transformed into a tornado shelter.

"Are the cats taking a shower, mommy?" Gracie asked. It's a very logical question, but I had no time for logic. I had to herd one adult, two children, and two cats into a bathroom the size of a phone booth and make it seem as if it's a perfectly normal and actually quite fun thing to do.

"Of course not, honey," I replied. "They're going to watch us play. Now, go get the pillows and blankets from your room."

Confused but always up for a little adventure, Gracie raced toward her room with her sidekick, Jack, obediently following behind. I started pulling the cushions off the sofas and piling them up in the bathroom. We have four sofas in our house, so I had quite a pile going in the tiny bathroom when the kids returned with their blankets.

"Are you cleaning the sofa, mommy?" asked Gracie.

"No, honey."

"But that's why you take those pillows off." She was right. Periodically, I remove all the cushions, hunt for spare change, lost eyeglasses, car keys, toy parts, and moldy food, then vacuum the sofas. My children always love it because it usually means they'll be reunited with long-lost toys, fuzzy candy, or suspiciously discolored cookies.

As Gracie watched me toss the last of the sofa cushions in the bathroom, she kept insisting that I clean the sofa. One thing about Gracie is that she insists on sticking to the routines of our house and takes pride in reminding me when I stray too far from the expected. I once again informed her that cleaning the sofa wasn't on the list right now, so she turned to Plan B—or should I say, Plan

J. She turned to Jack and informed him that mommy wasn't going to find his toys in the sofa. The words were barely out of her mouth before Jack's face scrunched up in that typical toddler fashion that's the precursor to whining, wailing, tossing one's self on the floor, and declaring the end of the world. Gracie knew the exact location of Jack's whine button. She pushed it and he revved up.

It didn't matter that there weren't any of his toys in the sofa or that I took the time to take him to each sofa to demonstrate the absence of any toys. The bottom line was they wanted the vacuum. The vacuum is the black dragon with the long sucking nose that sends my kids into fits of giggles. They have no interest in the regular vacuum I use for cleaning the floors and carpet, but when I bring out the smaller one for upholstery, the living room becomes a jungle adventure land. So if the cushions were off the sofa, the black dragon was expected to make an appearance.

I've read the parent manuals. I know you're not supposed to give in to a whining child. I know it reinforces the behavior and dooms you to years of future whining. Under normal conditions, I promise I would have followed those rules, but the sound and sight of hail the size of watermelons (news reports said golf balls, but I knew better) repeatedly battering my house was affecting my logic. So I gave in. To the closet I ran and dragged out the black dragon with the long sucking nose. Hoping the electricity would stay on, I plugged in the vacuum and did a quick six-second pass along the sofa. With the sofas "cleaned," I officially declared there were no lost toys and instructed the kids to get into the bathroom. They crawled over the mountain of sofa cushions and sat in the shower stall next to the two cat carriers. I piled cushions all around us and on top of the kids. The wind was getting stronger and within 10 minutes I heard the frighteningly unsettling sound of tree branches cracking and crashing to the ground.

My two cats started meowing incessantly. Whether it was due to the frightening sounds of the weather outside or the frightening situation of being in such close contact with two young children and surrounded by 50 pounds of pillows, I couldn't say. The kids, however, found it amusing and began meowing as well.

In my haste, when I placed the kids in the shower stall I forgot to pay attention to which child I positioned closest to the faucet. Putting Jack near the faucet would've been the wise move, but it was, unfortunately, Gracie who sat in the powerful position of having her hand resting on the water control. Being bored, hot, and always wanting to demonstrate how she can do things herself, I feared she would turn the knob and drench us, the cats, and my sofa cushions.

"Gracie, take your hand off the faucet knob, please," I instructed in my I Mean Business voice. Gracie's response was to slyly smile at me and tighten her grip on the faucet. I knew that if I just reached over to grab her hand, she would quickly turn the water on. She looked at Jack and then at me. At three and a half years old, she wasn't thinking about the consequences of her actions, nor was she thinking about any punishment she would receive. Right now, she was the older sister who was doing something that had the unblinking attention of an audience. Even the cats had stopped meowing and were paying attention. The only sound was the total destruction taking place outside the walls of my home.

"Gracie, take your hand off the knob, *now!*" said Authoritative Mommy.

"Why?" she asked.

"Because I said so!" said Mommy Dearest.

Gracie's hand slid off the knob and she sheepishly settled down in the shower stall.

After 20 minutes, the hail started to let up and the wind died down. We all stood up, crawled out over the sofa cushions, and left the bathroom. I went to the window and saw the sun starting to peek out from behind the clouds. And the sofa was clean.

Bob Evans to the Rescue

By Kae

In 1989 I moved to a small town south of Nashville with my three children. At the time, Matthew was five, Christina was three, and

Jessica was six months. My husband stayed behind in Chicago to sell our house. Why would I do such an insane thing by myself? Because I believed it was imperative that Matthew start kindergarten at the same time as all the other kids in his class. That way, he would not show up after all the little cliques were formed and be left out like Rudolph in the Reindeer Games.

Our house in Chicago didn't sell in time for the start of the school year, which is why David stayed in Chicago with the house and furniture and the job that was paying both mortgages and the bridge loan. I headed to Tennessee to our new house, which was devoid of furniture and lacked air conditioning, at the end of August with my three little bandits in tow. Matthew began kindergarten with his peers and we all waited for the house in Chicago to sell and daddy to join our merry little group. My husband finally arrived three months later, on Halloween night.

As many Friday afternoons as possible, we would pack our station wagon and head to Chicago to see daddy. The trip was nine hours door to door, barring any unforeseen events. On one of our early adventures, we made a discovery that changed the rest of our lives: Christina gets severe motion sickness.

Driving from Nashville to Chicago was a fairly easy prospect. There were three main cities that we had to go through: Louisville, which was one-third of the way there; Indianapolis at the two-thirds mark; and Chicago proper at the very end. Successful car travel with small children involves knowing how much to let them drink and timing the potty stops before entering any metropolitan area, where a cry of "I have to go potty" can lead to desperate attempts to cross multiple lanes of traffic to pull to a stop on the side of the road, allowing for an alfresco potty experience.

We had been traveling for about three hours when we hit the outskirts of Louisville. About 20 miles south of Louisville, we had stopped and used the potty. Matthew and Christina had played around a picnic bench to run off a little energy before the next leg of the trip. Traffic in Louisville was particularly bad this day and we hit creep mode. Matthew entertained all of us by describing the make and model of the cars we saw.

The kids had figured out that if they pumped their arms in the air as if they were pulling the string on the locomotive horn, a lot of the truckers, bored to tears with the traffic dribbling along, would blow their big truck horns. Christina enthusiastically pulled her chubby little arm up and down right next to the window to make sure she was seen. When she was rewarded with a blaring of the horn she squealed in delight, kicking her feet wildly until I had to tell her to stop kicking the back of my seat.

Baby Jessica was in her car seat strapped into the front seat, facing backwards and just enjoying the passing time. Remember, this was still the 1980s. We didn't have air bags in the car and the campaign to have all children ride in the back seat was still years in the future. Placing the baby in the front seat enabled me to feed her a bottle of juice, check the status of her diaper when necessary, and make sure that neither of her siblings was sticking anything up her nose, all without having to pull off the road.

Kentucky morphs into Indiana via a long iron bridge on the north side of Louisville. On this particularly hot, humid Friday afternoon, the traffic in our lane came to a complete halt less than a hundred yards onto the bridge. We were in the middle lane. Your choice of lanes when traveling with more than one child is not always dictated by your destination but because it's not fair if all the trucks are on one child's side of the car and not the other's. The traffic continued to crawl past us on both sides, creating a fair distribution of semi trucks and horn blowing possibilities, but also a very disturbing bouncing effect on our stationary vehicle.

"Why's the car jiggling up and down?" Matthew asked while pumping his arm frantically at the passing truckers. "Steenie, you missed that one. Keep your arm up closer to the window. Do it like this, watch me." Matt was the consummate first child. Christina was his minion and he took his job as big brother very seriously. He spent every waking hour making sure she was following the rules, doing it (whatever "it" was at the moment) correctly, and explaining things that he didn't think she completely understood.

"It's the weight of the trucks on the different sections of the bridge," I explained the bouncing.

"I only see one bridge," Matthew said.

"The bridge is like the skin on a snake. It has sections so that it can move when there is weight on it."

"Oh no, I don't like snakes on the bridge," Christina chimed in.

"No, Steenie there's no snakes *on* the bridge. The bridge *is* a snake."

"No, Matthew. The bridge has sections that are like the scales on a snake, to help it move," I said.

"What happens if we bounce off? We'll go right in the water and Steenie can't swim. "

"I can too swim. I have floaties." Christina said this while indignantly flapping her arms out from her sides to illustrate how the floaties worked in the water.

"Not in the car. We're going to bounce off and only me and mommy know how to swim." Matt was very sure of himself on the issue of swimming because he had taken swim classes in February at the YMCA and had learned to dog paddle. Christina had also taken swim lessons but still needed her water wings, a.k.a. floaties, to keep her head above water.

"Matthew, if this car goes bouncing off the bridge, we better know how to fly. It's a long way down to the water."

"Mommy, I don't want to stay on the snake bridge anymore." Christina said this with authority, and in the review mirror I could see her fold her arms across her little chest in the classic "the case is now closed" gesture.

"Unless this car can fly," said Matthew, ever the wiseacre, "we are just going to sit here forever."

"What do you think has stopped this traffic, Matthew?" I asked in an attempt to turn the conversation away from the two kids in the back seat. If left to their own devices, the subject of who can swim and who can fly would be debated ad nauseam on a sliding three-year-old to five-year-old scale for the next half hour, ending in one or both having a crying fit.

"I think one of these big trucks ran over the top of a little car and now there are people with their parts all over the road," Matthew offered.

"Oh no, snakes are on the road," said Christina of the one-track mind.

"And the worker guys are having to use their shovels to scoop them up," Matt added.

"Matthew, that is so gross. I think all the cows escaped from that cow trailer we saw before," I suggested.

"Cow says moooo." Christina had the See 'n Say toy that tells what all the animals say. This was her favorite toy and she was more than happy to share her extensive knowledge of animal vernacular.

"Yeah, maybe the leader of the cows picked the lock on the truck and let all the other cows out when the traffic first stopped," Matt suggested, forgetting that the escaped cows were likely the reason that the traffic stopped in the first place. I let this pass.

"Are there any baby cows on the snake bridge?"

"There are no snakes on the bridge, Steenie. There aren't any baby cows either; they are too little to go on the highway without their mothers."

"I think the highway patrol has called in for their cow-herding dogs," I said, once again pulling the conversation back from the sliding scale of three to five. It's never good to let conversations linger there.

"Doggies say ruff-ruff."

"Maybe the hold-up is because the highway patrol is flying in their herding dogs in helicopters," I said.

"Maybe they'll drop the dogs in parachutes," Matthew said hopefully, and immediately began watching the sky outside his window for helicopters and parachuting dogs.

Then I heard the sound that no mother under any circumstances wants to hear: the guttural noise a child makes as she unloads the entire contents of her stomach, followed by the splattering sound of hours of clean-up. As the sound filled our car, all conversation died on our tongues. Two more guttural explosions later, everything in my back seat was covered in Christina's half-digested lunch. The traffic in front of me began to creep slowly forward, so there was no way I could turn around and assess the damage.

"Are you okay?" I asked, trying to adjust the rearview mirror so that I could see Christina better.

"I trowed up."

"She threwed up on my coloring book and on my cars," Matthew lamented. "It's so gross. It's everywhere and it stinks. I can't breathe."

"Okay, settle down. Christina are you okay?"

"I trowed up." This time she said it as if I had not grasped what had happened. The sound of tears welling up was clear in her voice.

"Did you trowed up on your shirt?"

"Yes"

"And in your ears?"

"No"

"And on Matthew's coloring book and cars?"

"Yes, and on my shoes, and on the car seat, and on my pants, and on my arms, and on my socks, and on Matthew's pants..." Christina was now so involved telling me all the places she had "trowed up" that she had forgotten she threw up and was giggling her little head off.

"Steenie's got throw-up in her hair and everywhere. Gross! It went down the toy bag." Matthew began thumping about salvaging his toys and moving them to the other side of the seat.

The smell inside the car quickly became unbearable. We rolled the windows down all the way—on penalty of death if I saw any-one's hands even looking like they were going out the windows. That's all I needed was to have someone swipe an arm off while the car was full of puke. One crisis at a time.

The traffic was horrible. The afternoon sun was baking down through the metal beams of the bridge. The heat of the day that had been absorbed into the blacktop was being released back into the atmosphere and seemed to be focused directly under our car. We were surrounded on all sides by diesel trucks spewing foul fumes into the air. The little puffs of breeze pushed the fumes in through the open windows to mix dangerously with the noxious fumes already inside the car.

After what seemed like an eternity, the traffic began to inch slowly forward. Finally our car was expelled into Indiana. I slowly made my way into the right lane. Exit after exit went by. One thing large cities are notorious for is that the areas right outside the city directly on the interstate can be a little bit "rough." The last thing

I was going to do was take an off-ramp into an unknown intercity area at dusk with three kids under the age of six, one fully covered in her half-digested lunch.

We drove down the interstate with the windows rolled down, thankful for the fresh air billowing into the car. Christina, having fully recovered from whatever that was all about, was back to pumping her chubby arm in the air to get the truckers to blow their horns, her sneakers covered with her undigested lunch leaving tiny little tread prints on the back of my seat.

Finally, seeing an exit with a Bob Evans restaurant, I drove off the interstate, down the ramp, and into the parking lot. The parking lot was full. Cars were coming and going, backing in and pulling out. There was movement everywhere. All the "before the cow traffic jam" people had finished their meals and were leaving fat and happy. All the "after the cow traffic jam" people were pulling in to soothe the hungry beasts they had become during their involuntary detention.

I parked the car and told the kids not to move. I grabbed the diaper bag, got out of the car, and opened the back door on the driver's side, where Christina was. I was now able to assess the damages. The report was not good. The heat of the day and the delay in being able to begin the clean-up had conspired against me to create a situation where slime had rapidly hardened into crust. Sitting in the back of my Ford Taurus station wagon with the gray cloth interior was one child in a car seat covered from head to foot in her lunch. The hair on top of her head was sticking straight up, making vomit the strongest styling product on the market. On the floor were the puddles that had dripped and dropped while I was driving. Matthew was more than correct: Christina had thrown up not only on his coloring books but down into the toy bag that was sitting between them on the seat. His shoes and legs and socks were splattered. His shorts and shirt had little dots of half-digested food here and there.

I had no towels, no washcloths. All I had was a small travel-size box of baby wipes and one plastic grocery sack. This was not going to do it. I went to the back of the car and opened the hatch. Surely I would have something in all this stuff to help me out. The sun was quickly going down, leaving me standing in the semi-dark parking lot of Bob Evans on the edge of the interstate, six hours from the nearest bathtub, wondering what in the world to do.

One lesson learned on this trip was when packing the back of a car, you have to pack for every conceivable crisis. I had just thrown stuff in the back of the car without thinking. When my crisis was upon me, I found out that packing all the kid's suitcases behind the multiple heavy boxes I planned to have my husband pull out on the other end was not so smart. So there I was, sitting in a quickly darkening parking lot with a six-month-old baby, a three-year-old covered in vomit, and a five-year-old who, in his opinion, had lost all his worldly possessions, and the only two bags that I could reach were the diaper bag and my own overnight bag.

Matthew had begun to lament that the car stank and he needed to get out. I opened his door but he said that was not enough air, he was suffocating. I told him he was not going anywhere just yet because I did not want him to get squashed in the busy parking lot.

I took Christina out of her car seat, stood her on the parking lot pavement, and stripped off all her clothes. Off came her shoes, socks, shirt, shorts, and underpants. There she stood in all her natural glory underneath the sodium vapor parking lot lights. I pulled a T-shirt out of my overnight bag, fitted it over her head, and pulled her arms through the holes. The T-shirt hung down to just above her ankles. I used her shirt to wipe as much vomit as I could off her shoes, then I put them back on her sockless feet.

I stood her and her brother next to the car and told them not to move. I turned her shorts inside out and used them to wipe the vomit out of the bottom of Christina's car seat, then wipe off the straps and the front lap bar. I swiped at the seat and ran everything I could down onto the vinyl floor mat. I pulled the floor mat out and wiped everything into the small plastic bag. I put all the clothes into the bag along with the ruined coloring book and other paper items in the seat and tied up the ends. The plastic bag, along with the toy bag filled with vomit, ended up in the garbage pail by the front door of the restaurant.

Jessica had fallen asleep during the traffic jam but began to wake up when I turned off the car engine. She was still just an infant and had only two modes of operation: sleep and eat. Since she had just been asleep, she assumed it was time to eat and began the preliminary feed-me fussing.

My goal in life was to be the best mother possible. The circumstances surrounding the birth of my first child curtailed any desire I had to consider the option of nursing. The birth of my second child was much more traditional and allowed me the luxury of nursing. I was determined to breast feed all further children no matter what. Everything you read in those days said breast feeding was the best way to feed your new baby. Your child would have healthier bones and a heartier immune system if you breast fed. I think I had even read that your child would be better "adjusted" if mother's milk was given early and often. While in theory breast feeding works out well, there are times when it is terribly inconvenient. This was proving to be one of those times. I had a small bottle of juice in the diaper bag for just this sort of situation. But Jessica was not to be fooled. This wasn't her mother's breast and it surely wasn't her mother's milk. Now she was not fussing but shrieking her indignity at the attempted ruse.

With as much of Christina's lunch as possible removed from the children, our motley group of four made its way to the restaurant front door. I was hoping this would be one of those restaurants where the bathrooms were in the front just near the entrance. We could just sneak through into the bathroom get some paper towels and hot water and everything would be fine. But this was not to be.

Did I mention that the restaurant was packed? Did I mention that the baby was shrieking? The hostess did not ask me what I wanted or what I needed. She simply informed me that the bathroom was through the main dining room in the far back right-hand corner. So there we were, weaving our way through the maze of tables and booths, attempting not to bump into or make eye contact with any of the diners: the mother whose hair was more than slightly mussed and who would not realize until everything was over that she had had a smear of vomit on her left cheek, carrying a car seat on her jutted-out hip containing a shrieking infant, with a diaper bag slug over the opposite arm to create the proper counterbalance to keep her from listing dangerously to the left, holding the hand of a very small, adorably cute little girl with "trow up" making her hair stand straight up on her head like she was scared senseless, wearing a T-shirt hanging to her sockless ankles with her tennis shoe laces flopping in all directions because her mother, in her haste, had failed to tie them, trailed by a quiet, serious little boy with splatters on his clothes and his favorite Hot Wheels cars held in his hands out in front of him as if he was paying homage, hoping they would be cleaned in the bathroom sink.

Finally, in the women's bathroom, the shrieking baby in the car seat was set on the floor, the T-shirt-clad girl was stripped naked again and the boy waited patiently with his outstretched hands for his turn. I started the water running and laid Christina on the counter with her head toward the sink. We played beauty parlor. I was the washer and she was the customer. We washed her hair and sang the hair washing song. (This is not an actual song but just a melody I make up on the spot at each hair washing adventure. Just a little la-la-la to take the children's mind off the fact that they really don't like to have their hair washed.) When the water ran clear, I sat her up and squeezed out the excess water.

As luck would have it there were no paper towels in this bathroom. On the wall was the hot air blower that was intended to provide a more sanitary experience. I put Matthew in charge of pushing the button. He tried it out a few times to make sure he had the idea. This was okay by me—it would mute the sound coming from the baby. I stood Christina in the sink and proceeded to wash her down like a baby zoo animal. Then I stood her under the hot air blower, instructing Matthew to hit the button every time it shut off.

Between turns of pushing the button on the hot air machine, Matthew put his cars in the sink and used copious amounts of hand soap to clean out all the parts. He made sure to spin the wheels and open the doors and the hoods. Soon he was engrossed in the play of it.

Finally, I turned my attention to the shrieking baby. My milk had let down and now I was rapidly soaking through the breast pads in my bra. Since my daughter was wearing my extra shirt, leaking through this one wasn't a good idea. I provided the baby with her dinner while I sat on the floor of the bathroom with my back to the wall and watched my naked child dance like a ballerina under the hot air jet and Matthew play swamp monster rally in the sink.

Attempting to take a break, a waitress happened in on our little party. Seeing that I had my hands full, she brought both the kids a to-go cup of juice and me a Coke. Life was glorious after all.

Final Thoughts

What Matters Most

By Pam

People who are unfamiliar with adoption often ask me what it was like to see my daughter and son for the first time. Many of them confess that the thought of adoption scares them because they aren't sure they could unconditionally love a child who isn't biologically theirs. I think they have it all backwards. What amazes me is that our children love *us* unconditionally despite all the mistakes we make as parents. Regardless of whether the children are ours biologically, by adoption, or through remarriage, they trust that we'll chase away the monsters under the bed, heal all boo boos with our magical kisses, be their biggest champions and turn them into productive members of society.

God creates families in many different ways. From the moment I held Gracie and Jack in my arms, I knew beyond a shadow of a doubt that they were as much my flesh and blood as if I had physically given birth to them. Adoption is not for everyone, and you need to do a lot of self-examination to be sure you're emotionally ready for that journey. I knew I was ready to adopt children, but what I wasn't prepared for was how much those two little children would love me in return. Despite my mistakes and flaws as a mother, they're stuck with me and they don't seem to mind that one bit. They are my reason for being.

When I hold my children in my arms, my world is complete. The sound of their laughter melts away all my stress. When we play hide-and-seek, they help me find the child in me. I often forget that my children are adopted.

When I look back on life before Gracie and Jack, I wonder why I felt it was so important to have everything in its place. I wonder why it mattered that my hair was neatly combed and my makeup was perfect. Why was it so important to be wearing matching shoes? Why did I enjoy having a purse that couldn't possibly hold two sippy cups, extra diapers, wipes, tissues, hand sanitizer, and a snack bag of cookies? Did I really need more than five hours of sleep? What was the point of paying extra for stain-resistant carpet if you weren't going to try to get stains on it?

Even though I'm always the oldest mother on the playground and some people assume I'm Jack and Gracie's grandmother, becoming a mom at a mature age has been quite a blessing. My children keep me young. When we go to the playground, I know I'm the only 50+ woman going down the slide, climbing the monkey bars, and crawling through the tunnels, but I don't want to miss those precious moments. I see some of the younger mothers sitting on the benches texting or talking on their cell phones as their children play alone. I think of how much they're missing. I don't want to miss anything. I waited too long for the precious gift of motherhood and it's already going by too quickly.

I know I've made mistakes in raising my kids and I will undoubtedly continue to make them. Gracie and Jack may very well end up on a therapist's couch someday complaining about their mother's behavior. But there's one thing they'll always know for sure: They are very loved.

The Ride of Your Life

By Kae

When I began my journey into motherhood, I assumed that raising children was like a bell-shaped curve. You started out at the baseline of your emotional life and, by virtue of having a child, increased the vertical emotional trajectory until the child entered his middle-school years. At that point you began to get ready for the fast approach of college and the decline of the emotional trajectory of your life, until at the day you dropped your child off at college and returned to the baseline of your life before children.

After 27 years of raising children, my perception has changed dramatically.

Now I know that raising children is like riding the roller coaster at the New York New York Hotel in Las Vegas. Your first pregnancy is like walking steadily forward in a line that snakes around and gets imperceptibly steeper with each step. Finally you reach the front of the line and board your particular randomly selected car for the roller coaster ride. Like the birth of the child, you are expelled out the door. The first drop provides the momentum for the entire rest of the journey.

You are treated to a fast-paced trip of ups and downs, zigs and zags. Just about the time you get used to the speed, you are thrown into a few loop-the-loops in rapid succession. You alternate between being exhilarated and terrified. You laugh uncontrollably and then scream like a banshee. The last ups and downs spit you out into the tunnel approach to the finish. Finally, you disembark in a place that is nowhere near the place you were when you got on this roller coater.

Some people come out of the tunnel after the ride ecstatically giving each other high fives. Some are smiling with tears streaming down their faces. Some are shaking and crying, swearing they will never get over the adventure. Some are just stunned into quiet contemplation. I came off this ride as one of the exhilarated.

About Two Imperfect Mothers

Pam Johnson-Bennett

P am and her husband, Scott, have been married for 13 years and have two children, Gracie (age nine) and Jack (age seven). Also in the family are three cats and a dog. When Pam isn't driving her kids to school, dancing lessons, or baseball, she works as a certified animal behavior consultant. She is the author of seven books and has made numerous national TV appearances. Pam is a former vice president of the International Association of Animal Behavior Consultants and currently heads up the cat division for that organization. Pam is also on the Advisory Board for the American Humane Association. She writes the *Think Like a Cat* blog at Yahoo's new site, Shine.com, and is also the cat behavior expert for Friskies, where she writes a weekly blog at Friskies.com. Previously, she was the awarding-winning behavior columnist for *Cats* magazine. She was also the behavior columnist for Yahoo, ivillage, The Daily Cat, and *Cat Fancy* magazine's web site, Cat Channel. Pam has won numerous awards for her writing.

Kae Allen

Kae is an accountant who lives in Tennessee with her husband, David, and their female Goldendoodle, Fred. Kae has three children, Matthew (27), Christina (24), and Jessica (21). Kae has spent the past 20 years building her own accounting practice, restoring an antebellum home, and raising her three wonderful children. Now that the years of car pools, homework, baseball games, and gymnastics meets are over, Kae spends her free time bowling and playing golf with David. Kae loves to bowl. She is the secretary for two leagues and the association manager for the women's local bowling association. Kae and David are enjoying their voyage into empty nesting, spending time in Florida and traveling as much as possible.

Acknowledgments

Thank you to Linda Roghaar and White River Press. Thank you to our editor, Beth Adelman, for your talent and guidance.

Pam: Thank you to my husband, Scott, for pretending not to see my imperfections as a mother, yet convincing me that those invisible imperfections should be made public through this book. Thank you to my two children, Gracie and Jack, for providing me with more joy and love than a heart can hold. I apologize in advance for any embarrassment this book may cause when it comes time for you to start dating. Thank you to my co-author, Kae, for being the true inspiration behind this project.

Kae: First, I want to thank my husband, David. Without his love, handholding, and creative input, my part of this book would never have been finished. Second, I want to thank my three amazing children. Without you there would have been no material for these stories. I appreciate you allowing me to write tell-all stories about your most private moments before the age of five. Third and certainly not the least important, I want to thank my co-author, Pam. Without your insistence, my part of this book would never ever have been put on paper for the world to read.

www.ingramcontent.com/pod-product-compliance
Lightning Source LLC
Chambersburg PA
CBHW030828090426
42737CB00009B/927